Essential Guides for
EARLY CAREER
TEACHERS

Mental Well-being
and Self-care

Essential Guides for Early Career Teachers

The *Essential Guides for Early Career Teachers* provide accessible, carefully researched, quick-reads for early career teachers, covering the key topics you will encounter during your training year and first two years of teaching. They complement and are fully in line with the new Early Career Framework and are intended to assist ongoing professional development by bringing together current information and thinking on each area in one convenient place. The texts are edited by Emma Hollis, Executive Director of NASBTT (the National Association of School-Based Teacher Trainers), who brings a wealth of experience, expertise and knowledge to the series.

There are three books in the series so far but look out for more as the series develops.

Essential Guides for Early Career Teachers: Assessment
Alys Finch
Paperback ISBN: 978-1-912508-93-8

Essential Guides for Early Career Teachers: Mental Well-being and Self-care
Sally Price
Paperback ISBN: 978-1-912508-97-6

Essential Guides for Early Career Teachers: Special Educational Needs and Disability
Anita Devi
Paperback ISBN: 978-1-913063-29-0

Our titles are also available in a range of electronic formats. To order, or for details of our bulk discounts, please go to our website www.criticalpublishing.com or contact our distributor, NBN International, 10 Thornbury Road, Plymouth PL6 7PP, telephone 01752 202301 or email orders@nbninternational.com.

Essential Guides for
EARLY CAREER
TEACHERS

Mental Well-being
and Self-care

NASBTT

Sally Price
Series editor: Emma Hollis

First published in 2019 by Critical Publishing Ltd

British Library Cataloguing in Publication Data
A CIP record for this book is available from the British Library

ISBN: 978-1-912508-97-6

This book is also available in the following e-book formats:
MOBI ISBN: 978-1-912508-98-3
EPUB ISBN: 978-1-912508-99-0
Adobe e-book ISBN: 978-1-913063-00-9

Cartoon illustrations by Élisabeth Eudes-Pascal represented by GCI
Cover and text design by Out of House Limited
Project Management by Newgen Publishing UK
Printed and bound in Great Britain by 4edge, Essex

Critical Publishing
3 Connaught Road
St Albans
AL3 5RX

www.criticalpublishing.com

Paper from responsible sources

Contents

Acknowledgements

Teachers who have accessed well-being coaching in their training and subsequent NQT years tend to keep in touch and report back how having experienced a safe space has helped them. The strategies within these eight chapters come largely from their inspiration and so I would like to thank them as well as my colleagues Matt Barnard and Kate Thirlwall and supervisor Nick Luxmoore. Inspiration from Hannah Wilson's strength and vision and transformational research from Sonia Blandford have empowered me to believe in the purpose of this contribution to the *Essential Guides* series. In addition, I would like to thank sincerely all the writers and thinkers acknowledged in the book. Sam Twistleton and Emma Hubball's support and encouragement have also been valuable and greatly appreciated.

The author and publisher would like to thank the following for kind permission to reproduce copyright material: Anna Freud Centre for Children and Families, British School of Coaching, endorsed by the Institute of Leadership and Management, Take to the Trees, At The Bus, Place2Be, Oxfordshire Mind, Oxfordshire Youth, Silver Cloud Health, Oxford University Hospitals' Here for Health service, The Energy Project, Suffolk and Norfolk SCITT.

I'd like to thank Josh Connolly, Maria Pattinson, Rachel Hunter and Kayleigh Loffhagen whose delivery and content during MHFA England instructor training resonated personally with me on many levels. Brenda McKay from the British School of Coaching has supported my thinking, particularly as I have developed as an active, non-judgemental listener, and has guided my positive unconditional regard.

Emma Hollis, Alison Hobson, Kim Francis and the NASBTT community have strengthened further my belief in the value of schools' role in progress for the better in Initial Teacher Training and I would like to thank my boss Patrick Garton (and all colleagues on our central team) for allowing me the freedom to explore and listen to so many great people working in this area. Patrick's forthcoming *Essential Guide* on *Behaviour*, will, I know, include the all-important link between mental well-being and behaviour and will support teachers in understanding why certain strategies do not work for certain people, and why other ones do.

Thanks too to Juli Beattie, Will Long and the rest of the At The Bus team (www.atthebus.org.uk) for their steadfast conviction on the benefits of art as therapy for whole-school communities, staff and young people and their families alike. Thanks also to Hannah Farncombe for her guiding light on both a professional and creative level. Lastly, thanks go to Will Price for reminding me of the importance of Schrödinger's cat.

Meet the series editor

Emma Hollis

I am Executive Director of NASBTT (the National Association of School-Based Teacher Trainers) and my absolute passion is teacher education. After gaining a first-class degree in psychology I trained as a primary teacher, and soon became head of Initial Teacher Training for a SCITT provider. I am dedicated to ensuring teachers are given access to high-quality professional development at the early stages of and throughout their careers.

Meet the author

Sally Price

I am a well-being and support officer and am on the central training team at Oxfordshire Teacher Training. I work in schools to support early career teachers with their mental health and well-being, and in teacher training locations with trainees, their mentors and programme leaders. Drawing on over 20 years of teaching experience in secondary and primary settings, I lead on well-being research and support and I am interested in the role and responsibility of employing schools in nourishing the developing autonomy of those new to the profession, as well as those who have been teaching for longer.

Foreword

As a passionate advocate of high-quality teacher education and continuing professional development, it has always been a source of frustration for me that beyond the ITT year, access to high-quality, structured ongoing professional development has always been something of a lottery for teachers. Access and support have been patchy, with some schools and local authorities offering fantastic opportunities for teachers throughout their careers while in other locations CPD has been given lip service at best and, at worst, is non-existent.

This series was conceived as an attempt to close some of those gaps and to offer accessible professional learning to busy teachers in the early stages of their careers. It was therefore a moment of genuine pleasure when proposals for an entitlement for all early career teachers to receive a package of support, guidance and education landed on my desk. There is now a genuine opportunity for school communities to work together to offer the very best early career development for our most precious of resources – the teachers in our schools.

The aim of this series is to distil some of the key topics which occupy the thoughts of early career teachers into digestible, informative texts which will promote discussion, contemplation and reflection and will spark further exploration into practice. In each edition, you will find a series of practical suggestions for how you can put the 'big idea' in each chapter into practice – now, next week and in the long term. By offering opportunities to bring the learning into the classroom in a very concrete way, we hope to help embed many of the principles we share into day-to-day teaching.

Teaching is the best job in the world. Teaching is also a very tough job. In my experience, entrants to the profession generally go in with their eyes wide open, expecting to experience the rough with the smooth – but even then, they are frequently surprised by some of the challenges they face. In too many instances, early career teachers become overwhelmed by the demands placed on them and flounder, losing sight of what attracted them to the profession in the first place. In this title on self-care, Sally Price walks you through some simple, practical approaches to taking care of yourself so that you can be the best possible teacher for the pupils in your care. Her message is really quite simple – teaching really is the best job in the world, but to enjoy it to the full you need to put yourself first.

I hope you enjoy exploring this book as much as I have enjoyed editing it.

Emma Hollis
Executive Director, NASBTT

Introduction

At 13 years of age, my friend Louise and I saw our music teacher, Mr Wallace, buying onions in Kwiksave. At the time, we thought the idea of a teacher buying onions was the most hilarious thing in the world. But, of course, teachers do buy onions just like the rest of us – and just like the rest of us, teachers have times in their lives when they don't feel so great. It is therefore important for you (and everyone else) to realise that, sometimes, it is ok not to feel great. It is even better if you understand what to do when that happens, and ideally have access to the tools to prevent it happening (as much as can ever be possible) in the first place.

This is an interesting title to write since, in my experience, teachers who require guidance on their self-care and well-being often will not allow themselves to seek help until it is far too late. All teachers need to practise self-care and look after their well-being. You might choose not to call it that, you might not know that's what you're doing, or you may not do it until it is too late. This book is responding to the fact that there are clearly many teachers who aren't in touch with what it is they need to do in order to stay well and happy in their jobs. This is particularly the case for those at the start of their teaching careers: *'between 2011 and 2017, the percentage of teachers leaving within three years' service increased from 20 per cent to 27 per cent, while the percentage leaving within their first five years increased from 27 per cent to 33 per cent over the same period'* (Rice, 2019).

Self-care is defined by the Brilliant Idea Studio as the maintenance of your immunity: physical, mental and spiritual (Rao, 2018). When looking at well-being, as an Early Career Teacher (ECT), you may usefully consider mental well-being as what is occurring internally as opposed to what might be externally visible to school communities. The World Health Organization defines mental well-being as the extent to which we feel cheerful, relaxed, active, rested and interested in life. Well-being is a keyword in the WHO definition of health: *'a state of complete physical, mental and social wellbeing and not merely the absence of disease or infirmity'* (WHO, 1946). MHFA England defines four stages of mental health need: whether you are coping, concerning, significant or critical in terms of your level of need; these judgements can be both subjective and objective. Having guided ECTs for many years as they find their way to the right teaching setting for them, I would argue that it is certainly worth prioritising your self-care and well-being needs in a preventative capacity alongside your responsibilities as a developing teacher. The consequences of not doing so are far-reaching.

This book hopes to demonstrate that, while it may seem contradictory, seeking support from others can often be the easiest way to discovering that the best solutions lie within your own self. Just as UCET's Schools' Reference

Group highlighted *'one of the hardest aspects in developing policy around mental health is to find balance. For example, between support and self-care... prevention and self-awareness and public and personal responsibility'* (Greer, 2018). But it is not impossible. The best way I have found to persuade those reluctant to engage with the idea of community responsibility for raised mental health awareness is to consider it not as a tool for *'indulging learned helplessness'* but rather as a tool for *'enabling self-agency'* (Price, 2019). Having worked for more than two decades within an arena of increasing school accountability and austerity, I have got to know 25 cohorts of staff, trainees and pupils. As I have listened to the frustrations of those learning to learn (both teachers and pupils) in large educational settings, two game-changing words keep cropping up – autonomy and control. I have become increasingly convinced that the frustrations faced by children in school as they struggle between needing support and paradoxically needing independence are directly comparable to the frustrations faced by adults in their early teaching career. Both pupils and new teachers are learning. Both need help. Both need to be trusted to own their learning. With careful support, both can flourish. With too much or too little support, both can flounder. In the eight chapters that follow, I present some solutions which are proving helpful to some teachers in some situations. Indeed, while community awareness and support are key, it is also useful to remember that everyone's mental health is unique.

From my own experience of working with local primary and secondary colleagues in recruiting and selecting trainees, and in consultation with colleagues across the country, it is evident that the teacher workforce is becoming increasingly diverse, supporting and reflecting the increasingly diverse pupil populations they teach. Diversity of ethnicity, gender and physical ability is subject to regional variation. What is accepted and welcomed in large-city school settings may not so readily be the case in coastal or rural areas, mirroring social patterns. Neurodiversity, however, while being represented in all pupil populations irrespective of location, is only now starting to be welcomed, valued and discussed within the teaching profession. A trainee teacher with whom I worked closely three years ago spoke out at a local meeting on mental health and well-being and then at national level for disabled teachers' consultation conferences. She is both brave and ground-breaking and represents the importance of the norm accepting the unique. Her pupils are extraordinarily lucky to have her as their inspiration. She has a chronic and managed mental health condition and teaches. She may be unique and she is by no means alone. Many serving teachers have similar diagnosed and undiagnosed conditions showing neuro-diversity.

My first teaching post started just after the death of Princess Diana. Since then, I have worked with a great team of colleagues; seen many come and go; seen young people at their best and at their worst; been bereaved a few times; experienced divorce, remarriage, miscarriage, brought up kids; bought onions. My first head of department dragged me to the communal staffroom and forced me to get to know colleagues. My second head of department taught me the power of humour. She has an enviable capacity to maintain a healthy philosophical perspective even in the most challenging of times. Latterly – rather than teaching young people – my role focuses on supporting teachers who train with us and who teach across primary, secondary, special and mainstream settings within the county. I've also been lucky enough to travel further afield, meet truly inspirational teachers and specialists and train and learn with many varied minds, all of whom have the same core motivation: that of giving young people the best possible start in life. With their support, these young people are therefore developing the best possible set of sustainable strategies to approach life's inevitable challenges. Some teachers do this by facilitating a passion for knowledge and a growing confidence and competence in their subject; some do this by supporting the development of social and coping skills; some do both. Firm yet nurturing support as young people grapple with burgeoning independence and the bumps on the way seems to be working well as a strategy for many of the wonderful people I have met. One of whom, Josh Connolly, ambassador of the National Association for Children of Alcoholics (NACOA), believes young people to be *naturally resourceful and whole*. I agree. And if this is true, then a teacher's role is arguably to support young people to engage with and acknowledge their resources, in order to find and enjoy a sustainable way of living and to tap into that resourcefulness. The most efficient way to do this? – active and overt role-modelling.

References

Conolly, J (2018) Plenary Talk. Paoer presented at Youth Mental Health First Aid Instructor Training, 13 March.

Greer, J (2018) *Boundaried Flexibility: Securing and Supporting the Best Mental Health in Our Trainees and Teacher Training Professionals*. Unpublished draft discussion paper presented at the UCET Schools' Reference Group and conference workshop, October 2018. [online] Available at: www.nasbtt.org.uk/wp-content/uploads/9-UCET-Schools-Reference-Group-Draft-Discussion-Paper-Mental-Health.pdf (accessed 17 August 2019).

MHFA England (nd) [online] Available at: www.mhfaengland.org (accessed 17 August 2019).

Price, S (2019) The Significance of Raised Mental Health Awareness to Support Teaching and Learning in Emotionally Healthy Classrooms. *Association for the Teaching of Psychology Magazine*, February 2019: 22–24.

Rao, S (2018) *Keynote talk for the Pennsylvania Museums Association conference in April.* [online] Available at: https://brilliantideastudio.com/selfcare/focusing-on-self care-is-good-for-business (accessed 18 September 2019).

Rice, P (2019) School Teachers' Review Body, Twenty-Ninth Report, 45 Crown Copyright (HMSO) 2019 – presented to parliament July 2019.

World Health Organization (WHO) (1946) *Preamble to the Constitution of the World Health Organization as adopted by the International Health Conference.* New York: WHO.

World Health Organization (WHO) (1998) *Well-being Measures in Primary Health Care/The Depcare Project.* [online] Available at: www.euro.who.int/__data/assets/pdf_file/0016/130750/E60246.pdf (accessed 6 August 2019).

Chapter 1   Core values and motivations for teaching

What? (The big idea)

Tap into what makes you tick!

It is only when you maintain connection with your core values and initial motivation for choosing to teach that you can sustain a purposeful approach to the demands of the job.

Teaching is great. You're never bored. No two days are the same. It is possible, with perceived pressure from all angles, to become disillusioned and to decide that working in school is no longer your bag. But there is hope, thanks to organisations such as the National Institute for Health Research, the Anna Freud Centre, Place2Be and MHFA England, who are working with ITT providers and partnerships between schools, Clinical Commissioning Groups and local school communities to pilot and map the impact of research-based interventions in improving the mental health of teachers and pupils. The findings of the University of Bristol's ongoing research, including that into the mental health of teachers set out first in the pilot study (2016) of the WISE project (Well-being in Secondary Education), allude to presenteeism as a major factor. This is in line with ECTs' concern over the unwritten perceived expectations to attend work even when ill – a mixed message not uncommon in parental communications home regarding the impact of absence on the performance of school-age children. Whether or not there will ever be parity between the 48-hour absence contagion rule of stomach bugs and the damaging emotional contagion resulting from presenteeism in cases of mental ill-health is for another time. The Deloitte study of October 2017 into the cost of presenteeism over absenteeism, mentioning that public-sector presenteeism contributes significantly more to days lost (89.8%) than absenteeism (10.2%), and MHFA England's reporting on the economic and social burden of disease brought about by mental ill-health means there can be little surprise that the place where everyone meets at some point or other is now targeted as the best place to sort things out – schools.

Lajos Göncz's 2017 review of psychological research into teacher personality since the 1940s points towards guidelines for a more comprehensive theory in educational psychology. While some ITT providers and employing schools favour a one-to-one proactive needs-based approach to supporting the personal and professional development of their trainees and school staff, requiring significant investment of time and energy, a growing number are looking towards more systematic mechanisms for supporting this personal and professional development. A number of providers and schools are finding studies of certain traits useful in predicting and supporting particular mental health and well-being needs and involving their ECTs in what this might mean for their self-care post recruitment. Irrespective of approach, increasingly ITT providers and employing schools are keen to develop preventative measures to save time, emotional energy and human resources. Göncz talks of the *'long-running consensus that the teacher's personality is the most important and complex variable in the educational process'* (pp 75-6).

It is known now that teacher personality and traits are not static and Göncz recommends bearing in mind the following: *'personality theory traits should not be treated as static, unchanging features... but rather as dynamic communicative styles, and it should be borne in mind that typologies are categorizations constructed for specific purposes'*. Also to be considered is *'leadership in small social group functioning as well as the guidelines offered by learning and developmental theories of pedagogical interventions that optimize students' potential'* (Göncz, 2017, p 91).

In a 1961 study entitled 'The Teacher as a Model', Adelson noted three types of teacher: the profession-driven teacher – demonstrating outstanding professional knowledge, teaching with charisma and narcissism and establishing a distance between themselves as experts and their pupils as ignorant learners; the student-focused teacher-facilitator – encouraging students to develop their own potential, demonstrating outstanding altruism and dedication to the profession, an exhausting and rarely successful strategy; and the institution-focused or values-based teacher whose teaching demonstrates complete devotion to a set of pedagogical ideals to the detriment of the spontaneity and independence of the students (Adelson, 1961).

In March 2018, Mike Culley, an occupational psychologist in the field of education, initiated discussions at the NEU regional conference *Promoting Teachers' Mental Health and Wellbeing* by introducing his research into the motivations behind applications to ITT institutions over the last 25 years. He found that those wishing to teach are likely to possess personality traits linked to those working in caring professions. These traits come with emotional charge and high-tariff energy use. Working initially with a Southend teacher training provider and as part of assisting in selecting and training teachers, he was involved in exploring the use of psychometric testing, post-selection, as a way of helping the trainee understand more about themselves and how they might fare during the course. He also helped others provide the right kind of target support where needed. The 16PF instrument (Cattell et al, 1970) proved 'less fluffy' than the Myers Briggs (MBT1) instrument in that it highlighted personality factors which may be considered indicative of trouble ahead, or significant challenge. There seemed to be three factors common in those successfully recruited and reaching QTS with competence and confidence. The three factors strongly noted were: 1) high rule consciousness – the desire to follow written and unwritten rules; 2) low vigilance – a trusting outlook, a positive view of human nature and low suspicion of the motives of others; and 3) a very high drive towards perfectionism. The proportion of trainees showing these three factors were well outside UK norm population scores.

Anna Richards and her ITT team across Suffolk and Norfolk are collaborating with the Relational Schools Network and the Relationships Foundation, with Cambridge Assessment and their Cambridge Personal Styles Questionnaire and with Dr Alison Fox's socio-mapping tool to support greater self-awareness and support for ECTs. They have harnessed the relationship significance for teacher longevity and have embedded a system to support overt focus and training in this area. Professional and personal networks, their size and quality, and the distance in these relationships can help to predict how individuals face challenges and manage them effectively. The Cambridge Personal Styles Questionnaire (CPSQ) measures coping, working with demands and relating to others, and behavioural competencies: caring and compassion, self-management and coping with demands all play a role in performance.

The key findings for Anna's context from cohort data from 2017–18 support the notion that the total number of positive relationships is pivotal. Those who tend to withdraw from ITT or early teaching tend to have had lower 'coping with demand' scores and those who are successful have had a positive relationship between ITT tutor and trainee. So it could be that the number of relationships correlates directly with the sustainability of the teacher's career in teaching. Whether relationships flourish or dwindle, whether they protect teachers from or exacerbate nascent challenges in early teaching experiences, has a pivotal effect on well-being and resourcefulness and therefore on the capacity for long-lasting self-care and self-empowerment.

While this isn't surprising, it is good to see that the overt implementation of strategies to identify and promote relationship training and #wellbelonging, a significantly pertinent term coined by Rob Loe of the Relationships Foundation, in ITT and ECT experiences works. In school settings which have been able to devote time and attention to ensuring ITT and ECT mentoring is fully resourced and supported at all levels, it seems the benefits are becoming clear.

In October 2018, Dr Julie Greer, Chair of the Universities Council for the Education of Teachers (UCET) Schools' Reference Group and headteacher of Cherbourg Primary, Eastleigh, drafted a discussion paper following the group's exploration of potential factors influencing the perceived increase in instances of poor mental health experienced by early career teachers. Greer's unpublished article on *Boundaried Flexibility* explains the importance of dual responsibility: of the teacher's own prioritisation of their self-care and of the supporting colleagues' responsibility in understanding and supporting any specific needs relating to poor mental health.

Your identity as a human being comes under 360-degree scrutiny during your initial years of teaching like no other time of your life. You are assessed and judged formally and informally by placement colleagues, training providers, young people in classrooms, parents and friends and family, the latter perhaps bearing the brunt of some of your worst days and forays into teaching, planning and marking. As you navigate your way through your early career, it can be common for you to lose sight of your identity and what it was that you held true about life and your purpose. You can become your worst judge during this time; negative self-talk is up there among the most common themes experienced by those supporting early career teachers as they reach crisis points during the year.

From reading Loehr and Schwartz's *The Power of Full Engagement* (2003), it seems likely that teachers, too, can benefit from engagement with and regular revisiting of personal core values in order to maintain and respect the role of self-care in a successful and rewarding teaching career. If you can dig deep, identify, articulate and revisit what it is that makes you tick as an individual, you are more likely to address personal questions which are key to your existence. You will be able to establish what it is about yourself that can be challenged and what it is about yourself that you will not compromise in order to survive the emotional storms you weather in your commitment to teaching today's young people.

So what? ◀ ◀ ◀

What does this mean in day-to-day terms as teaching practice develops?

Having visible reminders of your core values in your teacher planners or on a computer screen in your classroom can support your self-care when facing challenging tasks. There might, for example, be a difficult conversation with a carer scheduled. If a core value of 'family' remains at the heart of this difficult interaction, it may well be easier to remember that anger vented in our direction and frustration expressed during the interaction originates in a mutually held belief that the level of support from the primary caregiver in a young person's learning can be as influential as that of their teachers or peers. Remembering the role that both projection and transference play in your interactions with young people and colleagues can help to take the sting out of the emotional response and allow a protective perspective which can ensure the inner resources of emotional energy remain strong. Emotional vocabulary will be explored further in Chapter 3 of this guide.

Reflective task ◀ ◀ ◀

Applying your core values to professional challenges and workload management

Complete the purpose practice task using Figure 1.1 to investigate what's truly important to you.

- Add any important values not on the list.

- Choose the five most important to you.

- Take your time. Go from the gut.

Purpose practice: what matters to me?		
achievement	faith	knowledge
adventure	family	learning
authenticity	financial stability	loyalty
balance	freedom	power and authority
challenge	friendship	perseverance
commitment	generosity	recognition
compassion	growth	religion
concern for others	happiness	respect for others
courage	harmony	responsibility
creativity	health	security
curiosity	honesty	self-care
empathy	humour	self-respect
excellence	integrity	serenity
fairness	kindness	service to others
My five chosen core values are:		

Figure 1.1 Purpose practice: core values for resourceful teachers

(Based on the Deepest Values Checklist, *The Power of Full Engagement*, Loehr and Schwartz, 2003)

- Now take 15 minutes to reflect on barriers you have faced over the last few months as your teaching practice has developed.

- Consider your reactions to these challenges and the effect it has had on your attitude to work and on your professional relationships.

- Consider any steps you have taken to try to overcome the challenges and the outcomes.

- Have any of these steps included consideration of, or reconnection with, your core values?

- In looking for solutions now, can any of your core values support you in your thinking?

Case study ◀◀◀

Low mood and avoiding challenge

Consider the common barriers to well-being scenarios below, taken from the well-being chapters within the Oxfordshire Teacher Training ITT programme handbooks. These common barriers were recorded as a result of evaluations from three cohorts of trainees, central training staff and school partnership colleagues. The core value examples are taken from real situations in the last few years. The outcomes are those which have been reported back verbatim on anonymised sticky notes by ECTs in revisiting core values workshops.

Example   Applying your core values to overcome barriers

Common ECT barrier to well-being	Core value	Possible outcome
Unhealthy comparison with other ECTs.	Serenity: take a mental step back from the negative self-talk, talk with a trusted colleague/peer/ed support helpline and process the professional strengths you *have* been able to develop.	Improved ability to see the relatively small or negligent effects of another ECT's perceived superior competence or confidence on your own developing practice.
Fear of inadequacy in established team cultures.	Freedom: someone will have left in order for you to have taken up your rightful place in the team and yours is the freedom to establish how you fit in to that team, with guidance from others.	Mutual appreciation, by exchanging knowledge and expertise, of who brings what to the team in its new construct with you in it.

Common ECT barrier to well-being	Core value	Possible outcome
Personality clash.	Creativity: think of alternative ways of building positive relationships with the other person.	Some common ground in an unexpected mutual interest emerges during the daily mile round the school field at lunchtime.
Avoidance.	Balance: spend 30 minutes on the task you are avoiding, then 30 minutes reflecting on how it went – seek support if needed by setting it as a target.	Limiting your time on a task which has less perceived relevance to you can help retain perspective that is needed in order to get tasks done.
Feelings of isolation.	Family: establish a small community of school staff with whom you have a connection, following the model you have of your own family, and make time for them regularly.	Acknowledgement that it is possible and ok both to be happily joined to a group of people and also to find those same people at times intensely infuriating.

Now what?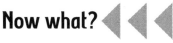

Practical task for tomorrow ◀◀◀

Following the purpose practice reflective task above, consider where visible reminders of them will benefit you in your working day. Write them on a sticky note. Put them in your planner, car, workspace; on your desk at school; in your phone; on your bike; as a screensaver; share them with your colleagues.

Practical task for next week ◀◀◀

Consider a task which you have been putting off. Does it fit with your core values? Does the reason for your avoidance or procrastination lie in the task not being aligned with your core values? Are there ways you can adapt the task, or your approach to the task, to enable you to engage more readily with it? In our well-being coaching room, we often remind ECTs who are frustrated at the differences of opinion they are faced with, that their colleagues will be unable to empathise with this frustration unless they are clear about the origin, or the 'this is frustrating me because', of the problem.

Take your teaching timetable. Write in each of your core values to demonstrate where they can be actively engaged with regularly each week.

Primary example — Keeping true to self during school

Mon	Tues	Weds – assembly	Thurs	Fri
Big write	**Creativity** Art/DT	Spelling	Literacy	PPA – walk off-site – **Freedom**
		Computing	Maths	Guided reading
	Maths			
Music		Maths	Science	Forest school
Phonics	Science	Guided reading		
Lunch outside whatever the weather.				
PE	Guided reading	History	Guided reading	PPA/
Serenity Class down-time – free choice well-being.	French	SRE	PE	Team meet + solo time **Balance**
Big write marking	Netball club	**Family** (family meal night)	Staff meeting	Marking

Mon	Tues	Weds	Thurs	Fri
Y8 French (a)	Y8 French (b)	Study support	Y9 German **Freedom** Class members sketch an emoji to typify what they were like when younger and/ or are free to choose a signature tune which demonstrates their past and present personalities.	PPA **Family** – drop kids at school
Y9 German	Y11 French	Y11 French	Y10 German	PPA plan for Monday
PPA **Serenity** Headphones on/music/ admin.	Y12 German	PPA **Balance** Go for a run + shower	Y8 French (a)	Y10 German
Paid lunch duty.				
Y12 German	Y10 German	Y8 French (a)	Y12 German	Y7 Spanish
Tutor period	Y9 German	Y8 French (b)		Y11 French film-making **Creativity**
Duty	Marking	Faculty time	Pastoral meetings/ marking	Marking + staff football, 5pm

Practical task for the long term ◀◀◀

Encourage your colleagues to engage with core values discussion when working on collaborative tasks. It can enable healthy distance from the focus, unlock previously untapped energies, and promote bonding – either by naming values in common, or by developing awareness of the different motivations between you. Wherever frustrations start to build resentment, check that you have tried to practise direct clarity with the colleague in question. By having the confidence to be clear about what it is that you need to change, and why, you are communicating purpose and agency. As Don Miguel Ruiz states in his *Four Agreements*: 'Find the courage to ask questions and to express what you really want. Communicate with others as clearly as you can to avoid misunderstandings, sadness and drama' (Ruiz, 1997).

What next?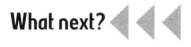

Further reading

Ashcroft, J, Child, R, Myers, A and Schulter, M (2017) *The Relational Lens.* Cambridge: Cambridge University Press.

Department for Education (DfE) (2018) *Recruitment and Retention Strategy (2018).*

Ford, T et al (2019) The Effectiveness and Cost-Effectiveness of the Incredible Years Teacher Classroom Management Programme in Primary School Children: Results of the STARS Cluster Randomised Controlled Trial. *Psychological Medicine*, 49, 828–42.

Hampson, E and Siegel, S (2017) *Mental Health and Employers: The Case for Investment.* Supporting Study for the Independent Review, 2017.

Kidger, J et al (2016) Teachers' Wellbeing and Depressive Symptoms, and Associated Risk Factors: A Large Cross Sectional Study in English Secondary Schools. *Journal of Affective Disorders*, 192, 76–82. [online] Available at: www.jad-journal.com/article/S0165-0327(15)30762-X/fulltext (accessed 17 August 2019).

Manning, J et al (2019) How Contextual Constraints Shape Mid-Career High-School Teachers' Stress Management and Use of Digital Support Tools. A Qualitative Study. *Journal of Medical Internet Research*, pre-print. [online] Available at: www.mental.jmir.org (accessed 17 August 2019).

MYRIAD: My Resilience in Adolescence Project. Oxford-based national research project on the impact of school-based mindfulness practice. [online] Available at: www.myriadproject.org (accessed 17 August 2019).

Suffolk and Norfolk School Centred Initial Teacher Training (nd) Relationships Matter – What Our Research Has Told Us about How Important Social and Professional Networks are for a Trainee Teacher. Blog post. [online] Available at: www.suffolkandnorfolkscitt.co.uk/blog/relationships-matter--what-our-research-has-told-us-about-the-importance-of-relationships-with-trainee-teachers- (accessed 17 August 2019).

References

Adelson, J (1961) The teacher as a model. *American Scholar* 301, 383–406 doi:10.2307/492944

Cattell, R, Eber, H W and Tatsuoka, M M (1970) *Handbook for the Sixteen Personality Factor Questionnaire (16PF)*. Champaign, Illinois: Institute for Personality and Ability Testing.

Culley, M (2018) Paper presented at the NEU Promoting Teacher Wellbeing regional conference, March 2018. [online] More information available at: www.mikeculley.uk (accessed 7 August 2019).

Göncz, L (2017) Teacher Personality: A Review of Psychological Research and Guidelines for a More Comprehensive Theory in Educational Psychology. *Open Review of Educational Research*, 4(1): 75–95.

Grant, A M (2017) Solution-Focused Cognitive-Behavioural Coaching for Sustainable High Performance and Circumventing Stress, Fatigue, and Burnout. *Consulting Psychology Journal: Practice and Research*, 69(2): 98–111.

Loehr, J and Schwartz, T (2003) *The Power of Full Engagement*. New York: Free Press.

MHFA England (nd) [online] Available at: www.mhfaengland.org (accessed 17 August 2019).

'Promoting Teachers' Mental Health and Wellbeing' Conference on Friday 23 March 2018, Kassam Stadium, Oxford – unpublished paper.

Ruiz, D M (1997) *The Four Agreements*, US: Amber-Allen.

Chapter 2   Coping mechanisms

What? (The big idea)

Build in your breaks, buddy!

Regular disengagement from work during the day = sustained ownership of job satisfaction.

The concept of 'strategic disengagement' from work has been around for a long time. Taking opportunities to 'refuel' in order to work more productively is not a new concept. In Loehr and Schwartz's ground-breaking work, *The Power of Full Engagement*, 2003, the benefits of engagement with core values and of short rituals of recovery interspersed between high intensity work, are clearly demonstrated. The concept of seeking regular and conscious departure from daily chores in order to declutter the mind and reconnect with the spirit has been around in many religious practices, such as Islam, for much longer.

Increasingly, some ITT providers are embedding aspects of this approach within their core programmes so that those joining the profession can pay conscious attention to their energy levels. For those working in school settings, it is easy to perceive expectations about output and performance as unrealistic. Bourdieu's 'doxa' theory is helpful in explaining why ECTs may struggle initially to gain clarity on what it is they can and can't do to own and therefore manage their time well during the school day. This perception can lead to a mindset of reluctance and limiting assumptions about the extent of what can be reasonably achieved within the working day, week or term. It is becoming increasingly clear, however, that adequate hydration, exercise, fresh air and daylight during the working day will significantly affect the level of ownership you feel about the work you do. In teaching, it may be beneficial to take note of the strategic breaks expectations of staff within the NHS and the perception that attention to self-care during the working day, in addition to outside it, is pivotal to a physically and mentally healthy working life.

So rather than avoiding taking breaks for fear of seeming weak or less committed, the new generation of ECTs is starting to play a pivotal role in a cultural shift towards mentally healthier schools. The Department for Education's new Early Career Framework (2019), in which *protecting time for rest and recovery* is named as something ECTs need to focus on when learning how to *manage workload and well-being*, suggests high levels of support for this cultural shift.

So what? ◀ ◀ ◀

What difference can this make?

Taking regular strategic disengaging breaks or short rituals of recovery (something which may previously have been construed in some school communities as being 'work-shy') have now been proven to impact positively on all aspects of physical, emotional, mental and spiritual health and well-being. This is reflected in the example provided by the new NHS Workforce Health and Well-being Framework (May 2018), which is now widely implemented for NHS staff. For those reluctant to see the relevance of this for teaching, the benefits can be linked to the current Teachers' Standards (TS) (see Table 2.1).

A note about trauma. For those teachers whose own lived experience of attachment was not straightforward, it is not always appropriate to recommend mindfulness. If only 56 per cent (Carlos, 2016) to 60 per cent (Moullin et al, 2014) of adults perceive themselves to have had attachments which were secure, then this supports the need for coping mechanisms to be down to personal choice. Whether or not coping mechanisms are a distraction from working through sensitivities or deep-rooted behavioural challenges, or an exploration of their provenance, it is important that mechanisms designed to help us cope with the demands of a chosen career in teaching are not imposed upon, but selected by, teachers themselves. That is why schools, appropriate bodies and teaching unions offering a range of recreational or creative activities is a good thing.

Following his inspirational talk at Oxfordshire Mind and Oxfordshire Youth's first Youth in Mind conference (2019) and in his chapter on a Muslim perspective on living well with good mental health, Imam Monawar Hussain (2019) talks of the *'dissonance between Muslim and Western understandings of mental illness'*. In the experiences I have had in working with ECTs who practise Muslim prayer, it is clear that, beyond the spiritual and religious devotion, it can contribute to living well and with good mental health. Taking oneself ritualistically out of the business of the day at regular intervals is beneficial to mind and body. Having a purposeful justification for cutting off from the day can result in the feeling that the burden of anxiety and stress has been lifted. ECTs may feel taking such a break during the directed time of the school day would be unjustified, but it is worth school communities supporting these regular breaks so that the directed on-task time is more efficient. As a result, the employee is wholly present during on-task time, as opposed to the jaded presenteeism reported earlier in this guide.

Table 2.1 How regular strategic disengagement can impact positively in schools

Reported benefits of strategic work breaks	Teachers' Standard impacted
More balanced perceptions of own competence.	Positive attitude role-modelling (1e).
Heightened awareness of self-care in others.	Effective communication on well-being (8e).
Increased focus and SMART work-rate which supports healthy work–life balance.	Plan, monitor, target-set from data (6c).
Clarity of response and timely reaction.	Know and cater for physical, social and intellectual developmental stages of children (5c).
Strengthened sense of purpose in role-modelling self-respect and autonomy.	Encourage pupils to be responsible and conscientious (2e).
Reconnection with original passion for subject.	Foster and maintain pupils' interest in the subject (3a).

Reported benefits of strategic work breaks	Teachers' Standard impacted
Sharpened perspective skills in instinctively and critically reflecting on learning progress in lessons.	Reflect systematically on effectiveness of lessons and approaches to teaching (4d).
Re-energised decisive and preventative approaches to behaviour management and reduction in need for reactive responses.	Maintain good relationships with pupils (7d).

For benefits such as these to be enjoyed, clear channels of communication are needed about best ways of working within the individual school context. There will be perceived unwritten expectations, as exemplified through Bourdieu's 'doxa' theory, in each staff culture about what is acceptable. Having these expectations outed through clear communication is something the ECT may need support with.

This is a specific example of how a robust and supportive mentor can be deployed. If ECTs are expected to make a positive contribution to the wider life and ethos of the school, then the employing school could usefully acknowledge openly that the ECT will be closer to the start of developing '...effective professional relationships with colleagues, knowing how and when to draw on advice...' (Teachers' Standard 8b) than more experienced colleagues. Engaging with teaching unions and with the appropriate body overseeing the induction process needs to be seen as professional and supportive linking and not merely a point-of-need contact. Seeking advice in a professional way beyond the employing school can ensure steps are taken early on to ensure support is targeted and useful for the teacher, and therefore ultimately for the school and its pupils.

In a practical sense, therefore, ECTs could usefully ask key questions of their colleagues in a bid to support establishing their own strategic disengagement routines, some of which will be answered during new staff induction by the school.

>> When staff are not teaching, what is the procedure for taking a break off-site during the school day?

>> In a bid to keep hydrated and refreshed during lessons, I will be drinking water and encouraging children to do likewise. What, if any, are the school policies I need to be aware of (children drinking in class etc)?

>> During the week, I am looking to access my healthy coping mechanisms (running, meditation, art class) in order to stay well. Before I book my classes,

it would be helpful to know the following: what are the expectations around the number of calendared evening commitments I need to attend and does the school provide any sports and social activities, or subsidised gym membership, for staff to support their well-being? Which nights do parents' evenings and directed team meetings happen?

Reflective task ◀◀◀

Applying your healthy coping mechanisms to your work schedule

Guidelines for positive mental health, promoted widely by CPD teaching unions such as the NEU's Mental Health Masterclass (Devon and Crilly, 2015), celebrate three key areas:

1. critical thinking;

2. emotional vocabulary;

3. coping mechanisms.

It is now widely accepted that time spent on conscious recognition of our own personal best-fit coping mechanisms is a worthy and integral part of self-care for school staff generally and particularly for the ECT. The three most effective and healthy coping mechanisms are:

1. mindfulness, meditation and yoga;

2. sport and exercise;

3. the creative arts.

These all have two common attributes, making them a successful ingredient in maintaining a teacher's self-care: they allow self-expression and they have intrinsic value and are distinct from all other activities whose purpose may be imposed by external factors (performance management, line management, target-setting, responsibility for dependents).

- Consider to what extent your working week accommodates regular engagement with your healthy coping mechanisms to ensure you are managing your well-being.

- Now note how your own typical week looks in terms of work tasks, cognitive breaks and alternatives worth trying, filling in the following table. An example follows in case you need some help.

Time	Work tasks	Cognitive breaks	Alternatives to try
Journey to school			
Time before seeing colleagues			
Time before seeing parents/ children			
Morning break			
Lunch break			
Between teaching and after-school commitments			

Example   My typical week

Time	Work tasks	Cognitive breaks	Alternative to try
Journey to school	Marking on the bus	Listen to audio book	Cycle one day a week
Time before seeing colleagues	Check work emails	Choose to meditate in class – place notice on door 'teacher meditation in progress' – sending strong self-care message to pupils and colleagues.	Set email responder to: 'my working day has now commenced. I will respond to your email by priority and in conjunction with my teaching and PPA workload today'.
Time before seeing parents/children	Mark work ready to show parents	Eat breakfast bar	Mark work in front of parents and talk them through your thinking.
Morning break	Break duty	Walking meeting	10 min jog round school field.
Lunch break	Paid duty	Walk to town	Play cards with colleague in sunshine.
Between teaching and after-school commitments	Input data before parents' evening	Yoga with key stage team	Drumming improvisation taster with neighbouring school colleagues.

Habitual

Sami was 27 years old when he started his SCITT programme and experienced a series of personal crises of confidence during the training year. He overcame these with a blend of:

» a support package from the central SCITT team;

» ongoing well-being support;

» some time out of the programme to reflect and regain perspective;

» re-focus on self-care.

He twice came to the decision that teaching was not for him, or rather that he was not up to the job. The majority of his closest friends had well-paid jobs in banking and finance, and when socialising with him at the weekend they struggled to understand why he had to limit his time with them in order to prepare for the next week's teaching load. Sami procrastinated about his lesson reflection and planning and became increasingly behind in this aspect of his work. This started to impact on his confidence and performance in placement schools and his colleagues began to raise concerns about his well-being.

Table 2.2 Coping mechanisms and effects

What were his coping mechanisms?	Effect?
Avoiding engaging in tasks which felt increasingly purposeless.	Increased backlog of tasks. Perceived inadequacy compared to cohort peers.
Absenteeism without explanation.	Increase in low mood. Decrease in self-worth. Loss of identity.
Isolation from colleagues and, increasingly, trusted friends.	Sleeplessness, chronic anxiety.

Sami is now in his third year as a qualified teacher and, while acknowledging he still has a lot to learn, approaches his teaching predominantly with a positive outlook. So what changed to turn things around? How did Sami tackle those unhelpful thoughts and how did these changes lead to QTS and positive job satisfaction?

Table 2.3 Coping mechanisms and benefits

What were his coping mechanisms during recovery?	Benefit?
When things got so bad that the thought of coming to work started to manifest in physical symptoms, Sami contacted the well-being team. After the session, Sami drafted an email to the Programme Leader – checked by the well-being coach – who then worked together with Sami to form an action plan...	Release from isolation.
... two weeks' time out from the programme and visit to GP advised*.	Ability to regain perspective – re-engagement with self in guilt-free setting.
Sami started to go back to the gym.	Low mood less frequent.
Choosing a variety of supports, rather than just one.	Increased perspective from previous hopelessness
Managed carefully when to see friends.	Boundaried relationships leading to more quality time with loved ones.
Touched base regularly with well-being coach.	Increased confidence in articulating and processing previously stuck emotions which had impinged on classroom performance and ability to plan efficiently.

What were his coping mechanisms during recovery?	Benefit?
Reconnection with reading as spiritual support: • Marcus Aurelius, *On Meditation*; Mark Williams, and Dr Danny Penman, *Mindfulness: A Practical Guide to Finding Peace in a Frantic World*, 2011; • Donald Schön, *The Reflective Practitioner, How Professionals Think in Action*, 1983; • Stoic Daily App – www.pocketstoic.com.	Confidence that struggles can pass and that with regular attention to spiritual needs, you can keep a connection with the self and be in tune with purpose for tasks and the original personal motivation for choosing to teach.
Morning ritual of positive self-talk.	Transforming anxiety into excitement about the day ahead.
Engagement with an NQT buddy.	Reminder not to over-think or over-work things; lesson plans could arguably always be better. Perfection comes with a cost and is unsustainable – an important message to role model to his pupils.

Now what?

Human nature prevents teachers being perfectly happy physically, mentally, environmentally and spiritually all the time. Yet there are practical ways in which you can take note of the aspects of your life which contribute to a generally healthier outlook. If you start to feel unwell, you can use these aspects; during periods of illness perhaps reassess your coping mechanisms, and during recovery be mindful of where and how things slipped. In this way, recovery management can be self-driven, with supports where needed. In well-being coaching training, relapse management is emphasised as an integral part of provision for clients.

In recent years it has proved useful for the teachers with whom I have worked to consider how their energy is shared between the 12 areas of the well-being self (see Figure 2.1). More often than not, teachers come to see me for advice or to offload when their efforts have been focused disproportionately on work relationships rather than on those requiring attention outside work.

- Watch this short video on strategic disengagement: www.youtube.com/watch?v=QRjqGWLLgUY

- What does coping mean for you? Read the exemplar well-being self-assessment in Figure 2.1, developed as part of the Health Creation Programme and incorporated into the British School of Coaching Well-being Programme, and then complete one of your own using the numbered headings.

Well-being diagnostic tool

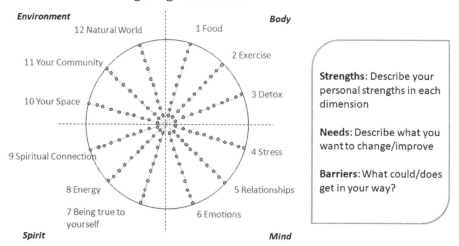

Figure 2.1 Well-being diagnostic tool

(British School of Co aching, 2009)

Example   Well-being self-assessment

1. **Food:** If I eat unhealthily the day before, I feel sluggish the next. If I plan in time during the week to prepare some fresh soup to sustain me through longer days (parents' evening; school production), I am more likely to stave off colds and this helps me deal proactively and positively in class with young people presenting with challenging behaviours.

2. **Exercise:** If I go for even a ten-minute run before having that glass of wine after parents' evening, I will sleep better and cope with the last day of the busy week.

3. **Detox:** Though I am conscious of the dopamine hit I get from answering all work emails and social media messages within an hour of receipt, I know that this is becoming too much of a habit, impacting on my real relationships. In my planner, I commit to one tech-free evening a week – and ask my friends and family to support me in this.

4. **Stress:** My positive work stress helps me perform with charisma in assemblies and with engaging teaching strategies when delivering some of my more successful lessons. In a full teaching day, I can feel on the cusp between tolerable and toxic stress. This is when I rant. I have nominated a class monitor to wave at me when they can see I'm nearing the 'rant' phase. It helps. We 'take five' as a class and discuss what could help us.

5. **Relationships:** At the start of the month, I've started to try and take time with family to highlight three sacrosanct evenings where we spend time together (swimming, dog walk, trip to the cinema). Things sometimes crop up, but this helps us have things to look forward to.

6. **Emotions:** I use the app *happynotperfect* most days in order to do two minutes' conscious breathing and naming of emotions and a gratitude exercise. This helps my work remain in a positive frame.

7. **Being true to yourself:** Having had some crunch points where neither my partner nor I felt we were having any engagement with ourselves as individuals and experienced loss of identity for the greater good of the family unit, we both arranged to commit to regular hobby time. He goes to the gym with friends one day a week after work and I paint on a Sunday morning with other artists in our village. In the classroom, I play my music at the start and end of lessons. Sometimes I invite playlist suggestions from others.

8. **Energy:** We weren't getting enough daylight, especially during the last term in the winter months. We have set our TV to go off after an hour and our dog helps us remember to take regular walks. It always makes us feel better and keeps the weight off (the dog's and ours!). The house is a bit messier, but we sleep well, having had fresh air.

9. **Spiritual connection:** I meditate on my bed for five minutes after work – sometimes this just means lying down in yoga pose and falling asleep – but this prevents the 'downhill slope' feeling of evenings. It gives me renewed energy for home life during the week each day rather than working myself into the ground and vegetating at the weekend.

10. **Your space:** In our house, we are constantly moving other people's things around to make room for what we want to do. I have given the garden shed a makeover so that some space in there is mine – I keep my stuff there and it stays out of other people's way. At school, we don't have designated personal space, so I take my headphones and a little pot of fragranced balm so that I can make a sensory space of my own when working on a specific task on any computer.

11. **Your community:** I tend to suffer from guilt – that my pupils don't get enough one-to-one feedback; that my kids don't get enough engagement from positive parenting; that my colleagues feel I am not pulling my weight; that my partner doesn't get much attention. I have found that through engaging in our local community together (eg charity pub quiz, local amateur dramatics, fundraising half-marathons etc), we get to spend quality time together *and* give something back to people in much greater need. It also helps us as busy teachers feel connected to our community – some of whom aren't aware of the extent to which we give constantly to our school communities at work.

12. **Natural world:** Being mindful of the change in seasons and caring for the small amount of wildlife at home helps me to connect with nature and to feel engaged in the cyclical patterns of life. This gives me strength in the belief that the hardest times are fleeting and that all things pass and rejuvenate. It's when I stop engaging with this natural momentum that I can feel overwhelmed with dark thoughts and helplessness. So I keep engaged with nature and collect eggs from the chickens.

Practical task for next week ◀◀◀

Read the example response below to the Anna Freud Centre's *Ten Steps Towards School Staff Well-being*, and then complete one for yourself related to the context of your own school setting.

Example   Ten steps towards school staff well-being*

Step	Content	Own school context	My part in this
1.	**Is there a staff mental health lead or champion who is responsible for coordinating the school's approach to staff mental well-being, and ensuring it remains on the agenda?**	*Yes – and a whole-school understanding that this does not excuse our own responsibility for self-care (Teachers' Standard 8b).*	*I am on the staff well-being committee representing new staff to help me engage with the process and feel my voice is heard – I am excused break duty once a month in lieu as an SLT goodwill gesture.*
2.	**Is there a mental health policy that addresses the needs of staff? Is it regularly reviewed? How is the policy embedded and communicated so that all staff are aware of it?**	*Yes – just been updated with the help of outside agencies – SDIP commitment to families and governor involvement in upcoming annual review.*	*Signposting in staff areas and on all screensavers. All departments have a standing positive mental health agenda item – colleagues take turns to share something which works for them – I have a whiteboard space in our department office where I can share weekly 'what rocks' and 'what sucks'.*
3.	**How does the ethos of the school promote openness about mental well-being and encourage staff to feel comfortable about sharing concerns?**	*We have developed a pre-meeting prep commitment – where colleagues mention a concern, they also suggest a solution in order that we tackle limiting assumptions around causes of concern together.*	*One of my transition targets from ITT to NQT was around time management – in department meetings, I'm responsible for time-keeping and ensuring tasks we are asked to do (eg work scrutiny; pre- and post-lesson discussions) come with a recommended time limit and review date. If we are unable to complete tasks in the time limit, we feed this back to our SLT-link and work with them on making tasks more manageable).*

Step	Content	Own school context	My part in this
4.	Are there opportunities for clinical and confidential supervision to help staff feel confident they are taking the right decisions when supporting pupils experiencing complex issues (including safeguarding and mental health, for instance)?	This is getting better. We have a regular Thursday after-school staff drop-in with our lead counsellor – this is increasingly well-attended and voice-recorded so that all colleagues can benefit from the advice as and when they have time to access it. Most concerns shared in the drop-ins are recognised as common issues, eg 'how to support a pupil experiencing a panic-attack for the first time'; 'what to say when you don't have time to listen for long'.	Next term I'm taking part in our cross-partnership supervision pilot – well-being leads in parallel schools across our partnership are supervising NQTs from groups of schools. We're writing up a confidentiality agreement with safeguarding and whistleblowing caveat. Then we're feeding back through our regional NQT appropriate body support team to local heads on strengths and next steps in terms of induction support for new staff.
5.	Could supervision be offered outside line management for those who do not feel comfortable approaching their manager with concerns about their mental well-being? Do staff know how to access external sources of support?	Yes – this already happens in some of our partnership primaries as a result of the SIP target from last review. The Education Support Partnership (www.educationsupport partnership.org.uk) have been really useful and we have an ex-colleague who is paid by the PTA to come in and run anxiety management workshops for any members of the school community (parents; teaching staff; support staff; pastoral teams).	Our new staff induction meetings and newsletters signpost us regularly to a variety of supports – some free, some paying, some available through their GP. We like www.hubofhope. co.uk and our local 'talking space plus' helpline.

Step	Content	Own school context	My part in this
6.	**Could measures to reduce workload or to limit hours spent working outside the school day be trialled – for example by reviewing marking policies and email protocols? Does the senior leadership team lead by example when it comes to limiting emailing at evenings and weekends?**	Our headteacher values our ownership of when individual staff choose to work – acknowledging some have childcare commitments and some choose to work late at school and leave home for down-time. We are encouraged to think of tasks which will benefit pupils most effectively, eg a 'common errors' starter or one-to-one oral advice with follow-up response time rather than spending hours writing the same comments in each book and pupils never having time for corrections.	Any emails I have had from senior leaders have been sent within the school day and have a guideline response time in the heading. I know some senior leaders write emails out of hours, but they delay sending out of respect for the recipient. I try to do the same.
7.	**Is there a comfortable, dedicated physical space within the school where staff members can take time out if needed?**	Our school is working on this – there is very limited space for staff and young people when they are engaging in work, let alone when they're not, especially at exam times – the well-being team is in discussion with Camerados who are piloting a public living room within our buildings next academic year.	We were trained on our SCITT programme to take every opportunity to get fresh air and daylight whenever we can during the school day. So I've got a reputation for requesting as many meetings as possible outdoors – even with a brolly! It helps me stay sane...

| --- | --- | --- | --- |
| 8. | Are there opportunities for staff to participate in activities with colleagues that are not linked to their work (for example, social events, exercise classes, or creative groups)? | We get subsidised swims at the local sports centre if we show our school badge and staff yoga has a reduced price for trainees and NQTs. Lots of pilots (art as therapy, heartfulness etc come to our school). | I think you'll always get colleagues who prefer to keep work and play very separate, but it can really help de-escalate tensions between groups of staff if they do engage in opportunities together. For some reason, we seem readier to do this if there is a charity element to our activities – there's a lot of perceived shame about down-time and guilt that we're not working around the clock. There's always more we could be doing, but at what cost to our mental health? |
| 9. | Is it feasible to introduce a staff well-being survey, to help understand the key issues in your school, and the impact of any measures you are taking to support staff well-being? | There have been a few surveys with varying purpose and outcome (Keele; Carnegie Centre of Excellence for Mental Health in Schools; Edukit; Leuven scale; NHS online mood self-assessment quiz). There are some fundamental indicators of scale in our school such as % staff absence; long-term sick leave referral figures; staff retention figures etc but since this area is dealing with mood and emotions, we often talk of the 'weather' of individuals and year groups or areas within the school community. Our headteacher feels that since the impact of every other area of our work is evaluated so minutely, it would be a hypocrisy for us to be using our precious time monitoring this and they would rather we spent that time engaging with our self-care itself. | A happy school atmosphere is palpable – within the classroom (TS1, 7, 8) and within corridors, outside spaces and staffrooms. That's not to say there aren't differences of opinion or heated discussions, but we try to role model for young people how we can rebuild relationships with colleagues – even when we agree to disagree. |

Step	Content	Own school context	My part in this
10.	Is the mental well-being of staff an agenda item at staff and governor meetings?	Yes and our school believes in a non-hierarchical responsibility to looking out for each other. So governors and SLT can also opt in to supervision pilots.	To begin with, our head of department used to just say before AOB – 'any mental well-being issues?' and we'd not want to dwell on this in order to keep to time, but now we take it in turns to prepare an example of a challenge to our mental well-being and how we overcame it – seems to work well – we don't always agree, but we always come away with an approach we hadn't thought of.

*These examples are a culmination of practices shared with me across the partnerships of schools in which our well-being team collaborates.

Practical task for the long term ◀◀◀

Embedding regular disengagement from work into your practice over time

Spend the next fortnight at work considering your version of the following (Figure 2.2). Keep voice notes after each day in order to help you notice patterns about fluctuations in your positivity towards engagement in work. At the end of the fortnight, and using this example, create your own self-care plan complete with strategic disengagement time for addressing your own effective healthy coping mechanisms.

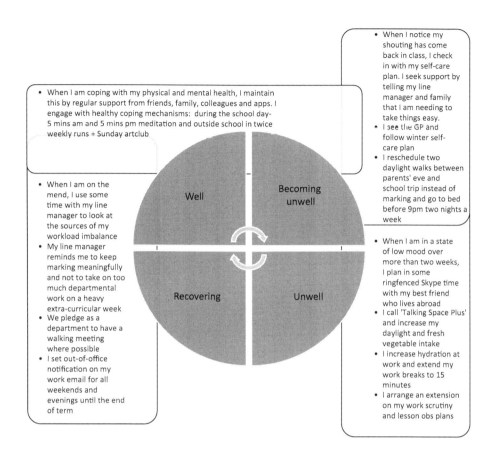

- When I am coping with my physical and mental health, I maintain this by regular support from friends, family, colleagues and apps. I engage with healthy coping mechanisms: during the school day- 5 mins am and 5 mins pm meditation and outside school in twice weekly runs + Sunday artclub

- When I notice my shouting has come back in class, I check in with my self-care plan. I seek support by telling my line manager and family that I am needing to take things easy.
- I see the GP and follow winter self-care plan
- I reschedule two daylight walks between parents' eve and school trip instead of marking and go to bed before 9pm two nights a week

- When I am on the mend, I use some time with my line manager to look at the sources of my workload imbalance
- My line manager reminds me to keep marking meaningfully and not to take on too much departmental work on a heavy extra-curricular week
- We pledge as a department to have a walking meeting where possible
- I set out-of-office notification on my work email for all weekends and evenings until the end of term

Well

Becoming unwell

Recovering

Unwell

- When I am in a state of low mood over more than two weeks, I plan in some ringfenced Skype time with my best friend who lives abroad
- I call 'Talking Space Plus' and increase my daylight and fresh vegetable intake
- I increase hydration at work and extend my work breaks to 15 minutes
- I arrange an extension on my work scrutiny and lesson obs plans

Figure 2.2 Cycle of health

What next? ◀◀◀

At the start of this chapter, we discussed that regular disengagement from work can support sustained ownership of positive job satisfaction. The relevance of this concept for you is particularly important, since the approach to work which you choose to take can have profound and silent impact on the children and young people with whom you work on a daily basis. As the core message of the nurturing programme organisation Family Links reminds us, it is the social interactions witnessed by young people at home and at school which trump any parental, pastoral or curricular intentions. Your behaviours significantly influence those of the young people within your setting. In this way, caring for your own physical, spiritual, mental and environmental health before that of others is arguably the most powerful choice you make.

The signposts to further research and reading of interest which follow are intended to support you with those inevitable challenges which arise when working in school.

Further reading

Anna Freud National Centre for Children and Families (2018) Ten Steps Towards School Staff Well-being. [online] Available at: www.annafreud.org/insights/news/2018/11/ten-stepstowards-school-staff-well-being-resource-launched (accessed 6 August 2019).

Anna Freud National Centre for Children and Families (2019) #SelfcareSummer Launched to Support Investigation into Lifestyle Changes to Alleviate Depression and Anxiety. [online] Available at: www.annafreud.org/insights/news/2019/08/selfcaresummer-launched-tosupport-investigation-into-lifestyle-changes-to-alleviate-depression-and-anxiety (accessed 6 August 2019).

Anna Freud National Centre for Children and Families (nd) Schools in Mind. [online] Available at: www.annafreud.org/what-we-do/schools-in-mind (accessed 6 August 2019).

Cattell, R B and Tatsuoka, M (1970) *Handbook for the Sixteen Personality Factor Questionnaire*. Champaign, IL: Institute for Personality and Ability Testing.

Culley, M (2018) Promoting Teachers' Mental Health and Well-being. NEU conference notes, March 2018.

Family Links (nd) [online] Available at: www.familylinks.org.uk (accessed 6 August 2019).

Gilbert, P and Andrews, B, ed (1999) *Shame: Interpersonal Behavior, Psychopathology and Culture*. Oxford: Oxford University Press.

Grant, A M (2017) Solution-Focused Cognitive-Behavioural Coaching for Sustainable High Performance and Circumventing Stress, Fatigue and Burnout. *Consulting Psychology Journal Practice and Research*, 69(2): 98–111.

Hughes, K (2018) The Impact of Developmental Trauma and Toxic Stress. Charlie Waller talk, 17 July 2018, Aureus School, Didcot. [online] Available at: www.nurture-psychology.co.uk (accessed 6 August 2019).

Jackson, E (2008) Work Discussion Groups at Work. Work Discussion. *Learning from Reflective Practice in Work with Children and Families Karnac*: London, 51–72.

Kidger, J et al (2016) Teachers' Wellbeing and Depressive Symptoms, and Associated Risk Factors: A Large Cross Sectional Study in English Secondary Schools. *Journal of Affective Disorders*, 192, 76–82. [online] Available at: www.jad-journal.com/article/S0165-0327(15)30762-X/fulltext (accessed 17 August 2019).

Meins, E (2017) Overrated: The Predictive Power of Attachment. *The Psychologist*, 30: 20–24.

Mental Health First Aid England (nd) *Stress Container Model*. [online] Available at: https://mhfaengland.org/mhfa-centre/resources/address-your-stress/stress-container-resourcedownload.pdf (accessed 6 August 2019).

Moullin, S, Waldfogel, J and Washbrook, E (2014) Baby Bonds: Parenting, Attachment and a Secure Base for Children. [online] Available at: www.suttontrust.com/wp-content/uploads/2014/03/baby-bonds-final-1.pdf (accessed 6 August 2019).

NHS Employers (nd) The Roadmap to Improving Health and Well-being. Oxford University Hospitals Staff Well-being and Self-care campaign. [online] Available at: www.nhsemployers.org/retention-and-staff-experience/health-and-wellbeing (accessed 6 August 2019).

NHS Health Scotland, University of Warwick and University of Edinburgh (2006) *Warwick-Edinburgh Mental Well-being Scale* (WEMWBS).

Oxfordshire Youth and Oxfordshire Mind (2019) *Youth in Mind Map 2019*. [online] Available at: https://oxfordshireyouth.org/wp-content/uploads/2019/03/YIM-MAP-DIRECTORY-HYPERLINKS.pdf (accessed 19 September 2019).

References

Carlos, V (2016) The Science of Adult Attachment: Are You Anxious, Avoidant, or Secure? *Elite Daily*, 22 February.

Department for Education (DfE) (2019) *Early Career Framework*. [online] Available at: https://assets.publishing.service.gov.uk/government/uploads/system/uploads/attachment_data/file/773705/Early-Career_Framework.pdf (accessed 19 September 2019).

Devon, N and Crilly, L (2015) *Fundamentals: A Guide for Parents, Teacher and Carers on Mental Health and Self-Esteem,* London: John Blake.

Emotional Health at School (2017) Why We Developed an Online Training Course about Student Mental Health. [online] Available at: www.emotionalhealthatschool.org.uk/blog-1/2017/11/29/why-we-developed-an-online-training-course-about-student-mental-health (6 August 2019).

Hussain, M (2019) A Muslim Perspective on Living Well with Good Mental Health. In Fletcher, J (ed) *Chaplaincy and Spiritual Care in Mental Health Settings*. London: Jessica Kingsley.

Loehr, J and Schwartz, T (2003) The Power of Full Engagement, Animated Core Message. [online] Available at www.youtube.com/watch?v=QRjqGWLLgUY (accessed 6 August 2019).

Moullin, S, Waldfogel, J and Washbrook, E (2014) *Baby Bonds: Parenting, Attachment and a Secure Base for Children*. [online] Available at: www.suttontrust.com/wp-content/uploads/2014/03/baby-bonds-final-1.pdf (accessed 6 August 2019).

Chapter 3 Emotional lexicon: which words work and when?

What? (The big idea) ◀◀◀

Using words well

If positive mental well-being is to be maintained, the ability to name and articulate barriers to positive mental well-being is a prerequisite. Being heard and understood is a crucial part of an individual teacher regulating a balanced perspective and processing challenging emotions which come with working under pressure in school environments.

Returning to the onions analogy of the Introduction, it can be useful to bear in mind that, alongside the professional responsibilities of a teacher are the personal responsibilities of that teacher, who is also a person. If, for example, your partner works for the emergency services, texts you when they get a shout, and then again to say all is ok – and this is a working model of communication which supports your relationship – this is going to have to be reassessed as you embark on your teaching career. How do you arrange for that communication to continue, while working with children and colleagues in an emotionally regulated and professional manner? How much you share of your personal circumstances will be dealt with more in the next chapter, but a discussion of the words you may wish to consider will start here.

The emotional energy taken to manage and absorb presentations and behaviours within the classroom from a range of young people is significant and requires processing. In her writing on the significance of the effects on those working closest with the most vulnerable children, Betsy de Thierry (2015) emphasises the need for teachers to voice and process as part of self-care in order to sustain their role.

> *For other emotionally involved professionals, the risk of compassion fatigue is recognised and support strategies are offered, but there is currently no acknowledgment of such a need for teachers, even though they are more involved and interact daily with traumatised children. Counsellors and psychotherapists have to complete a number of hours of clinical supervision in order to meet the regulation requirements.*
>
> (BACP, 2013)

She goes on to say how teachers, on the other hand, are often left without '*time to reflect, emotional support or an understanding of the nature and relational consequences for children and for others involved in those children's lives*' (p 126).

Pritzker also clarifies the importance of verbalising self-regulation to enable safety and readiness to learn. Both novice and experienced teachers should examine and reflect upon their own negative life experiences and support should be provided to process them in a safe and non-judging setting (Pritzker, 2012). De Thierry explains how in traumatised children of Type 3 classification, the part of the brain responsible for speech and language development (Broca's area) can be, in effect, closed down (de Thierry, 2015, p 102). ECTs who have experienced presentations of elective mutism may be aware of the misconceptions surrounding treatment of such behaviours. There are parallels to be drawn in the feelings of paralysis or inability to respond verbally by ECTs when faced with what they feel to be situations in which articulating a response is beyond their emotional range. In my experience, this is not normally when faced with young people, but rather when faced with colleagues who are responding to their practice before having empathised with the context.

New teachers tell me that, when they hit a problem, the difference between a good and a great mentor is the difference between sympathy and empathy, between the 'I'm glad I'm not you' and the 'I understand, I hear and I see how hard it is for you'. How much you are prepared to share about how you feel in school and how much you pretend that things are fine when they aren't depends on the level of trust which exists at cultural, team and modelled level. Do you work in a genuinely professional and accepting community where everyone's contribution is valued and the difference in contributions are applauded or do you work in a suppressed atmosphere of pretend excellence? Or a mixture of the two? In my experience, the key quality making a positive difference is that of approachability.

Natasha Devon's Mental Health Masterclass for the NEU in Birmingham in 2018 explored the three key guidelines for positive mental health, namely: critical thinking, healthy coping mechanisms and emotional vocabulary. It is useful to explore what types of opportunity arise for ECTs to name, articulate and process the arguably huge variety of emotions experienced within the school day. Containment of emotions requires regular release. How and where this happens within school premises is worth considering. What format reflection takes and how strong emotions are acknowledged, parked or allowed to come and pass can signify to what extent these emotions are controlled and regulated.

If the three key concepts for good mental health derive from critical thinking, healthy coping mechanisms and emotional vocabulary, what types of opportunity are you giving yourself as an ECT within lesson reflection to name and acknowledge emotions? How does this help you remain mindful that all emotions, positive or negative, pass and move on? How does this help build learner strength to cope with limiting emotions as and when they happen, and on reflection? This chapter will demonstrate simple, routine naming tasks which you can use in order to help 'park' emotional challenge in order to continue the teaching day's commitments in an emotionally contained manner, with the knowledge that time will be given later and when appropriate for processing.

So what?

What does this mean for your communication with young people, colleagues and families? While awaiting the introduction of mandatory professional supervision for those working with children in schools, it could be a real boost to your own positive mental health, during both term time and on well-earned breaks during school holidays, to set up your own sources of support to ensure a healthy regular offloading of emotional burden. It is fantastic news that the Early Career Framework advises ECTs to learn that both *'understanding the right to support'* is essential if workload and well-being are to be managed successfully, and that the fulfilment of wider professional responsibilities will include accessing *'expert support or coaching'*.

Some progressive partnerships of schools are already piloting peer-to-peer support where colleagues with similar positions across a multi-academy trust (MAT), for example, are meeting regularly to share, articulate and process challenges they face at work in order to maintain a healthy perspective and the ability to find solutions and coping strategies.

It is useful to spend time considering the verbal and non-verbal lexicon of the team into which you are inducted as an ECT. As well as familiarisation with established ways of speaking to collaborate, it is also useful to consider the subtext.

There are many similarities between strengthening the emotional resources of young people and those of teachers in their early career. Both are vulnerable and both have their daily work scrutinised. In line with Nick Luxmoore promoting the importance of developing cultures where *'it's normal for people to get heard but not by shouting louder than anyone else'* (Luxmoore, 2014), it is equally as important for those people to practise the ability of articulating what it is that they would like to be heard. Where a young person may be struggling with the what and why of their feelings, a teacher will do well to be clear on what it is that is causing them anxiety and why it is relevant that colleagues are made aware of this as soon as possible. This is a professional necessity if new teachers are to have any chance of staying in teaching.

Table 3.1 How emotional vocabulary can support sustained motivation and colleagues' ability to provide appropriate support

Challenge	Vocabulary	Outcome
Pupil swore at me	At the time I struggled to separate the young person's behaviour (and projection of their frustrations about what was happening for them) from a personal attack on my ability as a teacher – I took it as lack of respect for me, when it clearly was not all about me. I was so offended that I couldn't bring myself even to talk with colleagues about it.	I went home and drank three glasses of wine, internalising how useless my staying up the night before had been in order to mark in so much detail and plan a redraft lesson specifically with this young person in mind...
	Which words work and when?	
	I can see that this is difficult for you right now. I am looking forward to getting it right for you when these difficult feelings have passed and you feel ready to let someone help you see a way through. I'll come back to this space in a little while to see how things are.	Pupil sees that they have been listened to and learn that adults also find things challenging and use some time away to help them feel better. Pupil also knows they will get support, just not straight away owing to clear message from teacher.

Challenge	Vocabulary	Outcome
Sixth-form pupil in distress	Come on, time to get to lessons please, Year 12! **Which words work and when?**	Pupil's isolation and anxiety is perpetuated.
	I can see that you are in need of support and that is important. I am about to teach now and can see you at 12.10 if you come to the staffroom.	Pupil knows they will be given time and can de-escalate emotions owing to that knowledge. I can teach knowing that I have done what I can so far.
A looked after child (LAC) new to Year 5 class refuses to speak after hitting a fellow pupil.	Not again! We don't accept that at this school – why did you do it this time? **Which words work and when?**	Pupil has verbal confirmation that they are not worthy of their place here.
	This was hard for you and I can see we haven't got it right yet. How about you tell me how it feels and I can try to understand.	Pupil can see a way out of hard and heightened emotions without being told everything will be ok. They can see the grown-up is accepting they are struggling and is holding the emotion, not belittling it.
(cf. PACE model of intervention to regulate the soothe, threat, drive system and cycle of toxic shame in children living with repercussions of developmental trauma; de Thierry, Hughes, Gilbert and the Cornerstone Partnership and Emotional Literacy Support Assistant training)		

Reflective task ◀◀◀

In Ericsson's Deliberate Practice Model (Ericsson et al, 1993) six steps are deployed to support greater achievement: get motivated; set specific, realistic goals; break out of your comfort zone; be consistent and persistent; seek feedback; take time to recover. When faced with a lesson which didn't work as planned, or an interaction with a young person which did not end as hoped, ECTs learn the importance of reflection. The quality of this reflection – how much time is afforded; how open and honest the account is; whose support is sought in order to move on and learn – can influence greatly the resourcefulness of the teacher and the trajectory of either progress or regression over time of that teacher's practice.

- Reflect on your last challenge or personal target. To what extent does your experience fit with the deliberate practice steps listed above?

Case study

Applying your emotional lexicon in practice

A teacher with whom I worked on a regular basis during their ITT programme and NQT induction year learned through trial and error the importance of the ability to park emotional load in order to get through the teaching day after challenging circumstances. The skill of emotional parking links to an inner *resource* rather than *resilience*. The reason why I find the concept of resilience hard is that so many of the ECTs I have worked with have taken this to mean the need to suppress frustration and negative feelings and present a hardened exterior. This same ECT refers to resilience as a 'silly pretence'. For some, false resilience can eventually lead to burnout or an explosion of resentment or worse. If you can see *resourcefulness* as the aim rather than resilience, it can arguably feel easier to accept and self-permit recharging of resources and a more genuine and healthier relationship with the self and with work. Role-modelling parking to adolescents can support their self-managed regulation of emotions, rather than suppression thereof. As Luxmoore describes it, you can train colleagues and young people at school to 'wait their turn' in the knowledge that their troubles are worth hearing and important.

Now what?

Practical task for tomorrow

Naming and processing emotional challenges

Regular naming and processing of emotional challenges can support healthy energy management during the school week and term. At the start of class, ask everyone, including yourself, to draw an emoji of how they are feeling in the air. This allows an acceptance that there may well be a range of emotions, including your own, coming into the learning space and that each one is as valid as the next.

By doing the same at the end of the lesson, you are allowing an acceptance that responses to learning may well vary and that emotions can pass. It also frames the fact that you don't stop emoting at the entrance to a classroom and conversely it allows you to distance yourself from those emotions for the duration of the learning phase.

Practical task for next week ◀◀◀

Josh Connolly speaks convincingly about the ability for adults to create an atmosphere non-verbally, just by their emotional presence or absence in a room. Emotional energy, sometimes referred to as the 'weather' of a classroom or of a school, is good to gauge. More is said about adults owning emotions for the benefit of themselves and children in Chapter 5.

- Keep a note in your planner with an emoji for the weather of each lesson. To what extent were you responsible for this weather? What effect did this weather have on the learning which took place in class and on your emotions?

- Monitor whether your low mood affects that of the children in your class. If you perceive it to be happening, trial a pause from the lesson and engage in a short two-minute learning break in which the children have to try to make you laugh. They have to stick to the focus of the lesson. When the learning starts again, monitor any changes in the mood of the class and whether this affects children's readiness to learn or your readiness to teach.

Practical task for the long term ◀◀◀

Being aware of emotional energy in a room can also support long-term planning. Teachers are used to considering which elements of the curriculum work best at which times of day, week and term. Variables such as wet playtime (Hoyle, 1999) where children haven't had the opportunity of letting off steam outside; changes in seasons and classroom temperature; PPA being overridden by cover needs; unexpected visits to the school or classroom (wasps, inspectors, observers, new pupils) can all impact on this weather, but invariables, such as where PE falls within the day or hunger approaching lunchtime can be useful in informing or predicting the weather.

- Commit to keeping a regular note in your planner of what your anxieties are and where they are rooted. If you are unable to do this alone, seek one of your go-to people (see Chapter 7) and ask them to listen to you try and articulate it. Their task is to listen to understand, not to respond. Your task is to process through articulation.

Embedding regular connection with emotions into your daily practice

In an ECT's commitment to fulfilling expectations, it is common to find that development in practice is gauged by written documentation on many levels. Best practice I have observed has been where colleagues have explored alternative means of articulating progress and perceptions of progress other than through the written word. As emojis and snapshot symbols can be effective within the classroom to assess learning, so these can be effective for mentors, programme leaders, colleagues and ECTs themselves in getting quickly to the nub of the matter, in order to use time most effectively in supporting progress rather than in judging attainment. Manaz Pimple's daily reflection task with pupils living with a diagnosis of autism at Te Rise School Middlesex exemplifies the power of asking the emotional weather of the individual in a class setting in order to maximise readiness to learn (Pimple, 2017). At the recent series of NASBTT workshops on Establishing a Counselling, Well-being and MHFA provision for trainees, we shared current examples of practice in this area. One provider trialled a weekly emailed cartoon character for trainees to feed back on their week on placement. The year after, this was stopped, the year after that, it was resurrected following demand from placement colleagues and trainees themselves. This is an example of how something seemingly superficial and flippant in its simplicity can be pivotal in the crucial, yet potentially time-consuming, need for the individual to be heard and understood.

What next?

Further reading

Berliner, D C (2001) Learning about and Learning from Expert Teachers. *International Journal of Educational Research*, 35(5): 463–82.

Connolly, J (nd) How to Help a Child with Anxiety. National Association for the Children of Alcoholics. [online] Available at: www.nacoa.org.uk (accessed 6 August 2019).

Department for Education (DfE) (2019) *Early Career Framework*. [online] Available at: https://assets.publishing.service.gov.uk/government/uploads/system/uploads/attachment_data/file/773705/Early-Career_Framework.pdf (accessed 19 September 2019).

Elsa Support (nd) [online] Available at: www.elsa-support.co.uk (accessed 17 August 2019).

Erasmus, C (2019) *The Mental Health and Well-being Handbook for Schools: Transforming Mental Health Support on a Budget*. London: Jessica Kingsley.

Ericsson, A and Pool, R (1993) *Peak: Secrets from the New Science of Expertise*. Boston, MA: Houghton Mifflin Harcourt.

Fazel, M (2016) School Mental Health: Whose Problem? *Huffington Post*, 17 February. [online] Available at: www.huffingtonpost.co.uk/mina-fazel/childrens-mental-health-schools_b_ 9217164.html (accessed 6 August 2019).

Hoyle, T (1999) *101 Wet Playtime Games and Activities*. London: Routledge.

Luxmoore, N (2019) *The Art of Working with Anxious, Antagonistic Adolescents: Ways Forward for Frontline Professionals*. London: Jessica Kingsley.

McDonald, A (nd) Feel Brave. [online] Available at: www.feelbrave.com (accessed 6 August 2019).

McIntyre, N A and Foulsham, T (2018) Scanpath Analysis of Expertise and Culture in Teacher Gaze in Real-World Classrooms. *Instructional Science*, 46(3): 435–55.

McIntyre, N A, Mainhard, M T and Klassen, R M (2017) 'Are You Looking to Teach?' Cultural and Dynamic Insights into Expert Teacher Gaze. *Learning and Instruction*, 49, 41–53. https://doi.org/10.1016/j.learninstruc.2016.12.2005

Milne, T (2018) *Charlie Star*. West Sussex: Old Barn.

Palacio, J (nd) Digital Therapuetics for Mental Health Shown as Effective Intervention for Severe Presentations of Depression and Anxiety. [online] Available at: ww.silvercloudhealth.com (accessed 11 September 2019).

Pattimore, N (2019) It is Time Employers Brought Mental Health Top of Agenda. [online] Available at: www.peoplemanagement.co.uk/voices/comment/it-is-time-employers-broughtmental-health-top-of-agenda (accessed 6 August 2019).

Richards, D, Duffy, D, Blackburn, B, Earley, C, Enrique, A, Palacios, J E, Franklin, M, Clarke, G, Sollesse, S, Connell, S and Timulak, L (2018) Digital IAPT: The Effectiveness and Cost-Effectiveness of Internet-Delivered Interventions for Depression and Anxiety Disorders in the Improving Access to Psychological Therapies Programme: Study Protocol for a Randomised Control Trial. *BMC Psychiatry*, 18(1): doi:10.1186/s12888-018-1639-5.

Shotton, G and Burton, S (2018) *Emotional Well-being: An Introductory Handbook for Schools* (2nd ed). London: Routledge.

Sitler, H C (2018) Teaching Awareness: The Hidden Effects of Trauma on Learning. *Clearing House: A Journal of Educational Strategies, Issues and Ideas,* 82(3): 119–23.

References

British Association for Counselling and Psychotherapy (BACP) (2018) *Ethical Framework for the Counselling Professions*. [online] Available at: www.bacp.co.uk/events-and-resources/ethics-and-standards/ethical-framework-for-the-counselling-professions (accessed 11 September 2019).

De Thierry, B (2015) *Teaching the Child on the Trauma Continuum*. Guildford: Grosvenor House.

Ericsson, K et al (1993) The Role of Deliberate Practice in the Acquisition of Expert Performance. *Psychological Review*, 100(3): 363–406.

Luxmoore, N (2014) *Essential Listening Skills for Busy School Staff: What to Say When You Don't Know What to Say*. London: Jessica Kingsley.

Pimple, M (2017) Speech at Well-being Teachmeet conference. 10 October 2017. London: Digital Academy.

Pritzker, D (2012) *Narrative Analysis of 'Hidden Stories': A Potential Tool for Teacher Training*. Haifa, Israel: Gordon College of Education.

Chapter 4   Personal and professional self-care

What? (The big idea)

Careful what you carry

Youth MHFA England training teaches you the importance of self-care when working to support the mental health of young people. Containing, comforting and creating the conditions for children to come to their own conclusions is complex. Self-care sounds obvious and yet teachers so often comment on their colleagues prioritising the care of others over that of themselves. Being able to say no and to remain professional is not straightforward, and yet is essential for sustainability. The impact of social and professional relationships on the success of an ECT is profound. If you think that boundary-setting only needs to happen within the relationships between you and your pupils, time to think again.

Dr Tara Porter at the Anna Freud Centre summarises three key factors in what you can do now to ensure improvements in the mental health and well-being of young people and, by consequence, those who they look to for example: empathy, exercise and ethical responses (clarity over consent and confidentiality; Porter, 2019). It is healthy to call on a variety of sources of counsel for support. It is not healthy to exclusively offload the emotional baggage you acquire in the working week with loved ones outside the work setting, although they may need to know if you are struggling with a particularly sensitive issue. If you offload all your work baggage on those at home or socially, the propensity for empathy and compassion will wear thin. This is because listening is not a passive skill. It takes up emotional energy and emotional energy is finite.

Setting boundaries by defining yourself, not the child, is sound advice from Philippa Perry. Anthea Marris's workshops on the Art of Being Brilliant Parents are worth watching from a teacher perspective, not least to start to reconnect with the challenges of parenting at home, as well as to gain some insights about how strategies in your classroom might mirror best practice at home.

As explored in Chapter 1, Anna Richards and her ITT team in Suffolk and Norfolk are finding that their research with Relational Schools and Cambridge Assessment is so instrumental to better understanding the importance of self-awareness around relationship strengths and struggles that they have now incorporated their 'relationship proximity tool' as an integral mandatory element of the ITT programme. This, together with exploration of Dr Alison Fox's socio-mapping at the start, middle and end of the ITT year and the Cambridge Personal Styles Questionnaire, has helped them highlight a particular combination of maladaptive perfectionism, self-management issues and inability to cope with demands as the most common toxic mix leading to potential withdrawal from teaching. Social capital and relational capital matter and, as Anna says, it is logical when you think about it. However, it can be easily overlooked when the focus on subject knowledge development and classroom practice are prioritised. Yet, just as for young people, if relationships can be nurtured and are worth nurturing, this can, in turn, maximise readiness to learn, readiness to teach and self-empowerment. The term #wellbelonging coined at the Relational Schools Project is now taking on significant meaning for professional self-care by ECTs and pupils in their classes.

So what? ◀◀◀

Reflective task ◀◀◀

How much do you keep social and professional relationships separate? How much do you cut yourself off from social networks during term time? What, if any, effects do these factors bring about for your self-esteem and well-being?

- Complete the following table, noting the 'ideal' scenario and when there are exceptions to this ideal.

Boundary	Ideally	Exception to the rule
Where will you not do marking?		
Which times of the day will you not check email?		
In which places in school are you able to switch off?		
Which times in the school day can be set aside for you to focus on yourself?		
Do children know who they can turn to apart from you?		
What method of communication have you established with parents/carers of your pupils?		
How quickly do you respond to requests for information/deadlines/meetings?		

Case study ◀◀◀

Applying consideration of your relationships in practice

Eva has been training this year and has faced personal questions around her persona in school. Early in her first placement, she realised that while she didn't want to feel 'emotionally calcified' at work, she did want to develop a 'front'. She has since sought a combination of advice from placement colleagues who demonstrated to her the thought processes they might engage with prior to a lesson following some unexpected challenges at home or within their friendship groups: well-being coaching in order to rehearse how to remain professional but share with children in class when challenges are happening; seeking advice from experienced colleagues on migraine management and the effect it can have on anxiety and vice versa; returning to engagement with a previous talking therapy service with the assistance of Disabled Pupil Allowance. Eva is currently postponing completion of her QTS phase in order to access new drug trial solutions to migraine management and acupuncture to support alleviation of her symptoms, and she fully intends to return once this prioritised spell of self-care has enabled her to feel more agency around the aspects of her conditions and how this affects her mental well-being and fitness to work.

While in session, Eva and I reflected on the research and pilot studies of Dr Naira Wilson (www.thelittletherapyroom.com), who has been working with primary-aged children on preventative strategies to support their positive mental health with the metaphor of keeping their house in order. This is a useful preventative tool for building confidence in keeping your own ducks in a row as well as showing compassion to others and is based on a blend of acceptance commitment therapy and dialectical behavioural therapy. Eva could see the importance of working on her own self-care in order to best role model to young people too. It helped her arrive at permission to prioritise self-care by seeing it as helping others around her. Previously, she had felt compelled to plough on in a state of presenteeism in order not to let down the young people and colleagues around her. She has since seen the importance of taking this time out for personal self-care in order to better function professionally on her return to work in due course.

Now what? ◀ ◀ ◀

Practical task for tomorrow ◀ ◀ ◀

Freda Gonot-Schoupinsky has been researching the prescription of laughter to increase well-being in healthy adults, using the 'Laughie' – a self-care well-being tool. It is a user-created one-minute recording of the user's laughter, operated by re-playing it while laughing simultaneously.

- Create your own Laughie following the steps in Figure 4.1.

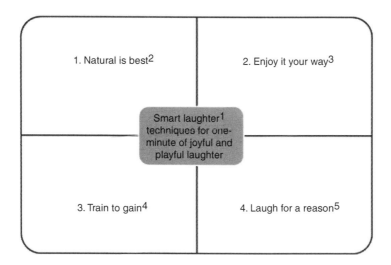

Note. 1. Smart laughter, laughing in a smart way, for a smart reason, on a smartphone. 2. Aim for a natural-sounding Laughie recording, and Laughie laughter. 3. For instance, you can add visual (eg a mirror), gestural, mental (eg thinking of joyful memories or amusing incidents), or social (eg sharing a Laughie) elements. 4. Practice and effort. 5. Meaning can include laughing for health, happiness, joy, humour, physical exercise, relaxation, meditation and energy.

Figure 4.1 Smart laughter techniques for Laughie usage

(Gonot-Schoupinsky and Garip, 2019)

Given that not all humour styles are positive (sarcasm and schadenfreude to name but two), this tool relies on laughter without the need to consider social influences on the object of the stimulus. That it can be self-created, and replayed by the creator; that there are no external boundary issues as it is a personally created tool for personal use; that it is accessible by those with long-term mental or physical health conditions and that it taps into the power of positive self-contagion culminates in a potentially ground-breaking, if simple, additional self-care tool. Initial studies show a unanimous positive increase in physical and mental well-being.

- Having recorded your Laughie, are you happy with it?

- Is your goal to listen to it three times a day?

- Do you have an idea of how you will remind yourself to listen to it (eg make notes in your diary)?

- What were you thinking of when you made your Laughie? Anything humorous, or just laughing, or a combination?

- Next week consider a challenge with which you are faced. Consider which of your five go-to people (see Chapter 7) would be best to ask for advice. Get in touch with them and see what they say. Get in touch with yourself and see what you say. Decide on your approach to tackling the challenge. Reflect on the part played by consulting your go-to person. Did it help? Would a different go-to person have been more appropriate to ask? Do any of your five go-to people need changing? Is there the right balance of work colleagues and friends and family outside work? Did you manage confidentiality regarding the challenge ok? Did you come away from the experience feeling that your asking for help or advice was met with empathy? How do you feel your relationship with that person has changed since you asked for help? Do they see you in a more or in a less favourable light? How do you feel about asking for help? Do you feel stronger about it now?

- Once your task is complete, use this to inform the wording for your own lanyard self-care plan.

- Create a self-care or WRAP (wellness recovery action plan) card for the back of your staff lanyard. When things get tough, have your own customised mantra to refer back to. Write down your five ways to self-care using the following five ways to well-being themes (Aked, 2008).

Example My five ways to well-being self-care plan

My five ways to self-care plan	
Take notice	Take notice of my basic needs and prioritise sleep regulation.
Be active	Hopscotch through the playground.
Keep learning	Learn from the wealth of experience that my appropriate body and teaching union can give me for free.
Connect	When was the last time there was mutually respectful yet spontaneous laughter in my classroom?
Give	Give my body the hydration and nutrition it needs.

Practical task for the long term ◀◀◀

Get enough sleep – carve out a non-negotiable eight hours sleep. If you have dependent family members, know that this is a challenge, but you can still have it at the back of your mind.

1. Aim for regular times to go to sleep and wake up. Keep these consistent even at weekends to promote healthy sleeping patterns.

2. Dim the lights and put away your devices at least an hour before bed. The blue light emitted by our tech device suppresses melatonin which is vital for sleep.

3. Keep your bedroom cool – around 18.5°C is optimal.

4. Avoid alcohol and caffeine.

5. If you cannot sleep, do not stay in bed. Instead read a book or meditate in another room in low light. Your brain should associate the bed with sleep.

Sleep. It isn't rocket science and yet so many of the staff well-being groups I have worked with, in both primary and secondary, special and mainstream settings have mentioned lack of sleep as a contributing factor in readiness to teach and subsequently, readiness to sleep – a cyclical thing.

That we have devised such creative – and even painful – ways of waking ourselves up in the morning says everything about how under-slept our modern brains are. Squeezed by the vise [sic] grips of an electrified night and early-morning start times, bereft of twenty-four-hour thermal cycles, and with caffeine and alcohol surging through us in various quantities, many of us feel rightly exhausted and crave that which seems always elusive: a full, restful night of natural deep sleep. The internal and external environments in which we evolved are not those in which we lie down to rest in the twenty-first century. To morph an agricultural concept from the wonderful writer and poet Wendell Berry, modern society has taken one of nature's perfect solutions (sleep) and neatly divided it into two problems: (1) a lack thereof at night, resulting in (2) an inability to remain fully awake during the day. These problems have forced many individuals to go in search of prescription sleeping pills. Is this wise?

(Walker, 2017)

And here are two useful links from Matt Walker.

» What happens to your body and brain if you don't get sleep? https://youtu.be/Y-8b99rGpkM

» Five tips for falling asleep quicker, according to a sleep expert https://youtu.be/ZKNQ6gsW45M

(Walker, 2017, p 281)

What next?

Further reading

Berry, W (1996) *The Unsettling of America: Culture and Agriculture*. California: Counterpoint.

Hayes, L (2015) *The Thriving Adolescent: Using Acceptance and Commitment Therapy and Positive Psychology to Help Teens Manage Emotions, Achieve Goals and Build Connection*. Oakland, CA: New Harbinger.

Jung, C (2003) *Four Archetypes: Psychological Types*. 3rd edn. London: Routledge.

Kline, N (2002) *Time to Think*. Washington, DC: Cassell.

Kline, N (2009) *More Time to Think*. Washington, DC: Cassell.

Louie, D, Brook, K and Frates, E (2016) The Laughter Prescription: A Tool for Lifestyle Medicine. *American Journal of Lifestyle Medicine*, 10(4): 262–7.

McKay, M, Wood, J C and Brantley, J (2007) *The Dialectical Behavior Therapy Skills Workbook: Practical DBT Exercises for Learning Mindfulness, Interpersonal Effectiveness, Emotion Regulation & Distress Tolerance*. Oakland, California: New Harbinger.

Marris, A (2019) The Art of Being Brilliant Parents workshops and *Resilience at Work*. [online] Available at: www.antheamarrisconsulting.com (accessed 6 August 2019).

Neves, L, Coredeiro, C, Scott, S K, Castro, S L and Lima, C F (2018) High Emotional Contagion and Empathy are Associated with Enhanced Detection of Emotional Authenticity in Laughter. *Quarterly Journal of Experimental Psychology*, 71(11): 2355–63.

Oxford Mindfulness Centre (2017). MYRIAD Project Study Details Published. [online] Available at: http://oxfordmindfulness.org/news/myriad-protocol-published (accessed 17 August 2019).

Perry, P (2019) *The Book You Wish Your Parents Had Read*. London: Penguin Life.

Rice Oxley, M (2019) Prevention: The New Holy Grail of Treating Mental Illness. *The Guardian*, 8 June. [online] Available at: www.theguardian.com/society/2019/jun/08/prevention-the-new-holy-grail-of-treating-mental-illness (accessed 17 August 2019).

References

Aked, J (2008). *Five Ways to Well-being: The Evidence*. [online] Available at: https://neweconomics.org/2008/10/five-ways-to-wellbeing-the-evidence (accessed 11 September 2019).

Gonot-Schoupinsky, F N and Garip, G (2019) Prescribing Laughter to Increase Well-Being in Healthy Adults: An Exploratory Mixed Methods Feasibility Study of the Laughie. *European Journal of Integrative Medicine*, 26: 56 64.

Porter, T (2019) Talking to Children and Young People About Their Mental Health. Paper presented at University of Hertford de Havilland Campus, Wellbeing Conference, 23 May 2019.

Richards, A (nd) Relationships Matter – What Our Research Has Told Us About How Important Social and Professional Networks are for a Trainee Teacher. [online] Available at: www.suffolkandnorfolkscitt.co.uk/blog/relationships-matter--what-our-research-has-told-us-about-the-importance-of-relationships-with-trainee-teachers (accessed 6 August 2019).

Walker, M (2017) *Why We Sleep*. London: Penguin.

Chapter 5 Solution-focused collaboration between parenting and pastoral care

What? (The big idea)

Plenty of parents got punched as pupils previously

Attend any continuing professional development course involved with engaging with families and the words *blame* and *fear* will emerge at least by the end of the introductory welcome.

The reason why an exploration of parenting and pastoral care is important in this guide on mental well-being and self-care for ECTs is that so much of what is expected of a teacher is to do with safeguarding procedure, and vigilance can predispose a tired ECT to emotional overload. The threat that 'it can happen here', as depicted in recent safeguarding campaigns around school sites, in staff toilets and in places where ECTs have lunch and breaks between lessons and directed time, and that things might be falling 'under the radar', can raise a compassionate teacher's working life to a state of constant hypervigilance. Lockdown procedure training and training classes of children in the same lockdown procedure is not for the faint hearted.

It could be easy to lose hope. A long-serving and highly acclaimed behaviour unit lead has seen it all and, during working hours – from breakfast time onwards – will act as primary caregiver for a whole host of devoted and vulnerable young people. She enjoys her career. It took a while for her to park her responsibilities and leave them at school for the evening and weekends to start with but, without doubt, she does good for every single young person with whom she works. While she is nurturing, she also believes in very firm boundaries. She is regarded by young people and school colleagues with respect. And yet the behavioural challenges she has faced in the last year or so have confounded even her: 'It's the downright *defiance* which is new to me, Sally'.

Since the criminalisation of corporal punishment in state schools happened a mere 30 years ago, it is understandable that some of the home-to-school frustrations are projections of a primary caregiver's own schooling. Given Family Links' belief that the most influential determinant of behavioural choices in young people is the nature of interactions between the adults they witness around them, it would seem a useful starting point to model how it is you want young people to behave by doing so at a parenting-meets-pastoral level.

However, part of adolescence, starting younger and younger, is the biologically necessary detachment from parenting figures in order to practise independence and gain self-sufficiency (Blakemore, 2018). This necessary friction at home and its ramifications for school, where young people project frustration on the nearest available substitute for parental figures, is one of the strands contributing to the potential increased emotional burden for ECTs with additional repercussions – the parent–teacher conversation.

While parents can fear societal condemnation of their parenting skills, and at worst, their children being taken into social care, the teacher, and particularly ECTs, can fear condemnation of their teaching skills. Some parents are deemed unfit to parent; some teachers are deemed unfit to teach. The part that mental well-being and self-care of parents and teachers plays in these judgements is significant. Where social supports for families and schools have dwindled owing to austerity, it is understandable how much despair exists. Channelling this into creating PTA-based social hubs after hours in schools where families and teachers can collaborate and be witnessed collaborating by young people is a productive use of energy and time.

Before questioning your practice in response to judgement from colleagues, parents and carers, reflecting on their motives and perspectives can help. Helping others speak about feelings will give them '*repeated relational experiences of feeling… worthy of compassion and concern'* (Sunderland, 2015) and in doing so, solutions are more likely to be welcomed and established.

Public health commissioners for mental health and parenting talk of the success of the Thrive programme in supporting young people and their families. Important here is the clarity on the duty of school professionals in safeguarding the confidentiality of mental health and well-being disclosures of young people and how this information is recorded and shared in order best to maintain trust and respect of the young person while ensuring adults working to support them fulfil their duties of care. Easier said than done. In encouraging young people to talk more, and in teachers searching for greater confidence and competence in listening, there is potential for additional conflict of responsibility here. The more you listen, the more, potentially, you are open to instigating safeguarding reporting procedures.

The Department for Education publication, *Keeping Children Safe in Education* (DfE, 2018), states that the Data Protection Act of 2018 and GDPR do not prevent or limit the sharing of information for the purposes of keeping children safe. *'Fears about sharing information must not be allowed to stand in the way of the need to promote the welfare and protect the safety of children'* (DfE, 2018, p 75).

The past 30 years has seen a change from legal corporal punishment in schools to its criminalisation. Whether or not we have sufficiently moved our alternative provision towards supporting young people to make healthy behavioural choices, it is fair to assume that it is not acceptable to utilise teaching strategies which promote fear and anxiety. Yet fear and anxiety can still be brought about by experiencing school. This is true for both pupils and ECTs. Parents and carers will have their own lived experiences of school. How to practise discipline in school and at home is a highly charged and sensitive area. Collaboration between home and school takes time and care. Is it realistic to establish a common ground? Is it possible to meet and discuss in a mutually respectful manner where everyone is a learner and judgement is suspended?

Since teachers and parents and carers were in school, have you really had a chance to meet and talk about what age-appropriate means nowadays? Given that it takes a village to raise a child, the potential role of Parent Teacher Associations in schools to develop the sense of capacity for promoting positive mental health is untapped. Sharing and owning information are not easy partners where supporting children's path to independence is concerned, but not sharing and not owning responsibility is not an ideal solution either. Where research meets social care, meets clinical provision, meets education, meets community is where good things are happening in school communities. Where Mental Health Green Paper Trailblazing Regions across the country are trialling how this meeting of agencies and perspectives might usefully work in practice, these discussions are moving sensitively and not without complexity, to a clearer shared understanding (McCotter, 2018).

So what? ◀◀◀

The impact on our ability to collaborate with colleagues, parents and carers

The fear of being judged as a new teacher is on a par with the fear of being judged as a parent or carer. Social services, while working incredibly hard to keep the most vulnerable safe, have a reputation of disruption and discord as it is often social services who are responsible for carrying out removal of children from birth parents. Appropriate bodies and disciplinary panels, in discussion with employing school colleagues, will decide upon fitness to teach and whether or not an ECT meets the requirements and expectations for teaching as set out in the Teachers' Standards.

In both parenting and teaching cases, the threat of exterior judgement, in legal terms, and potential removal from the opportunity to parent or teach a child, can itself lead to additional anxiety for some primary caregivers or teachers. Having preventative pastoral and community support for both parenting and teaching roles can support and guide in a positive and solution-focused way, and in preventing escalation to more punitive procedures can in turn alleviate the anxieties around perceived threat and judgement.

Discussions around best interests and safeguarding will be eternally problematic, just as there is a paradox for children who love their parents who hit them or who abuse each other. This is life and life is hard. Where conversations are encouraged around the impact of well-intended safeguarding measures on the mental well-being of children, primary caregivers and school staff, some genuine progress is being made. Where safeguarding has removed all agency and risk from children's lives, however, some genuine regression and damage to otherwise growing healthy independence is likely.

Table 5.1 Empathy over judgement

Judgemental response	Empathetic response	Outcome
'If the pupil is treated like other pupils without his complex needs, it will affirm his limiting assumption that he is intrinsically unteachable and not worth knowing.'	'It is clear to me from what you are saying that the repercussions of not reprimanding his behaviour are far more time-consuming for you and your team than if you were to follow procedure as with a child who has no complex needs.'	We can look to train together on awareness of presentations of this type while he has respite at the PRU so that when he returns, we are skilled to better respond when this happens again. www.thecornerstonepartnership.com
'When you email in to school on a weekly basis regarding your child's progress, you are taking away the opportunity for her to seek guidance from her subject teachers and she is learning that the locus of control lies with you not her, and therefore also, accountability.'	'I can see that you are wanting the best possible and informed outcome for your step-daughter. When her teachers next hand her work back, they will include some links to the resources you requested, together with a leaflet on constructing a mentally healthy revision schedule.'	The primary caregiver feels consulted and listened to and also sees that supporting learning can be done at arm's length rather than in the place of the daughter and that it could be more beneficial to support while maintaining the locus of control and independent choices as child-centred rather than parent-centred. This also enables school staff and primary caregiver to send the same message to the pupil that her choices are valued, respected and supported.

Judgemental response	Empathetic response	Outcome
'When you forcefully take Naira's coat off for her, she feels personally threatened and her ability to self-regulate the life-skill of getting dressed and undressed between outdoor play and indoor learning regresses. She may not be aware of how to conform to classroom rules, but she is acutely aware that you don't forcefully take anyone else's coat off and this supports her growing awareness that her difference from others is to be ridiculed and is shameful.'	'I can see that it is hard to manage this child with complex needs against demonstrating to other pupils that rules are to be followed. I wonder if, for the purposes of my own classroom management development, I might be allowed to try allowing the coat to stay on for the next week to see if the child's attendance improves? If I can find something to praise Naira for, I feel it might be a good way in to building a respectful relationship – this is one of my SEND NQT targets.'	Job-share colleague and ECT agree on a monitoring system where both have the opportunity to review the pros and cons of the approaches as part of the EHCP review. The progress takes time, and an interim compromise for Naira has been agreed that she now takes her coat off for class of her own accord, and keeps one glove on for the 'Big Write'.

Reflective task ◀◀◀

Consult with experienced colleagues for examples of challenging parental meetings and restorative justice conversations with young people.

- What did the colleague do in the meeting?

- How had they prepared?

- What happened as a result of the meeting?

- What records were taken and how was it followed up?

Case study ◀◀◀

Applying professional empathy in practice

A primary trainee teacher came to well-being coaching with a series of questions: What if children and young people's right to self-expression is being squeezed out of their schooling and home life, with less freedom to roam and discover academically and socially? What if, irrespective of the best intentions of today's parents/carers and teachers, their routes of self-expression become more suppressed and leak out in very targeted and toxic routes such as knife crime, self-harm, promiscuity and ultimately self-destruction, damage and mindless behaviour? And what if this leads to exclusion, arrest and contempt?

I nodded and let her continue.

The trainee recounted how a fellow teacher in a Pupil Referral Unit was looking after the most vulnerable looked after children and how a young lad, who repeatedly turned up late for school, was leaving the family home early to steal food for his younger siblings as his mother, high on cocaine in the flat opposite theirs, was unable to provide for them. The young lad was arrested for theft and his siblings were taken into care. In learning that theft was wrong, he started setting fire to himself as an alternative coping mechanism.

I let her continue, following Nancy Kline's 'time to think' approach. She had a lot to process.

When a young person feels comfortable enough to share with an adult and start their healing process, what does that adult do with the sharings? Are these very policies and procedures in place to ensure the safest start for children the very thing which is gagging free social interaction between children and the wider community?

The trainee had more.

The traumatic experience of being separated from birth parents can pale into insignificance with subsequent unsuccessful fostering and multiple care home placements. The traumatic experience of sustained child sexual exploitation can be greatly exacerbated by the need to speak in court faced with the aggressor. The trauma of domestic abuse can seem nothing compared to the forced reliving of this trauma triggered by an unwitting teacher wearing the same perfume as the violent parent. And so whose data is it? Who has the right to protect it? Do teachers have rights, as frontline workers interacting daily with young and frightened children, to know the information which could help them best provide for the child in class – what to say and more importantly what not to say?

We talk about DSLs and she is clear on procedure. We talk about the importance of shared responsibility. We talk about self-care and recovery from emotionally charged days at school. She talked with her colleagues more. She accessed a series of TalkingSpace Plus confidential phone calls. She is resourceful and whole.

Now what?

Practical task for tomorrow

Given that Teachers' Standard 8e requires you to communicate effectively to parents or carers on a child's achievement or well-being, consider a colleague, parent or carer whose choices around supporting a child you find relatively challenging. What unconscious bias might have been at play in previous interactions with them about this child? When going into a meeting with the child, colleague, parent or carer about the young child's achievement or well-being, what purpose does the meeting have for you? For the other people present? What type of listening occurred? Who had a voice? Where was blame apportioned and where not? What could be a way forward which does not rely on blame or judgement?

Practical task for next week

Consider an instance where you feel the parenting or disciplinary decision over a young person may not be in the best interests of the young person and may not turn out well. Instead of asking why, ask how the colleague or the parent feels. Try listening to understand, rather than listening to respond. Go in with the notion you are not there to fix the problem, but to support them in their own fixing, with you as an unconditional believer that they can – no matter how long it takes.

Practical task for the long term

A common understanding that we are all learners and that each adult invested in the child has opinions of equal value is problematic. While we all might feel we have the best interest of the young person at heart, it is ethically questionable that a school's behaviour policy is always better than any parenting strategy which the child may be exposed to. The difference is that behaving at home and behaving at school are different and this is the same for adults who work in school as well as for young people. Rules will arguably need to be tighter and more explicit in school, since this will be a place where scale and footfall is proportionally higher and therefore risk is greater.

Consider a theme around behavioural habits of young people, which often causes differing opinions to be raised in the staffroom or between home and school. Consider ways in which parents, carers and school staff could work together and learn together in a non-judgemental, mutually respectful setting to raise awareness, confidence and competence in dealing with the particular behaviour. It could be punctuality, sleep problems, mood swings, changes in friendship groupings or balancing outdoor activities with social media time.

What next? ◀ ◀ ◀

Further reading

Chamberlain, T (2011) Children and Young People's Views of Education and Policy, National Foundation for Educational Research. [online] Available at: www.childrenscommissioner.gov.ukhttps://dera.ioe.ac.uk/2692/1/force_download.php%3ffp=%252Fclient_assets%252Fc p%252Fpublication%252F483%252FChildrens_and_young_peoples_views_of_education_policy.pdf (accessed 11 September 2019).

Clinical Nurture Psychologists (nd) [online] Available at: www.nurture-psychology.co.uk (accessed 17 August 2019).

Emotional Health at School (nd) [online] Available at: www.emotionalhealthatschool.org.uk (accessed 17 August 2019).

Family Links (nd) [online] Available at: www.familylinks.org.uk (accessed 17 August 2019).

Future Learn (nd) [online] Available at: www.futurelearn.com (accessed 17 August 2019).

ONS/NHS (2018) Mental Health of Children and Young People in England, 2017. [online] Available at: https://digital.nhs.uk/data-and-information/publications/statistical/mental-health-of-children-and-young-people-in-england/2017/2017 (accessed 17 August 2019).

Oxfordshire Youth (nd) [online] Available at: www.oxfordshireyouth.org (accessed 17 August 2019).

Price, S (2019) The Significance of Raised Mental Health Awareness to Support Teaching and Learning in Emotionally Healthy Classrooms. Association for the Teaching of Psychology Magazine, February 2019: 22–24.

Rogers, J (2010) Facilitating Groups. London: Open University Press.

Sunderland, M (2015) Conversations That Matter: Talking with Children and Teenagers in Ways That Help. London: Worth Publishing.

Tuckman, B W and Jensen, M A C (1977) Stages of Small-Group Development Revisited. Group and Organisation Studies, 2(4): 419–27.

Walter, J (2016) Why I'm Glad Corporal Punishment is Now Only Found in Books. *The Guardian*, 1 July. [online] Available at: www.theguardian.com/childrens-books-site/2016/jul/01/corporal-punishment-jon-walter (accessed 17 August 2019).

Young Devon (nd) [online] Available at: www.youngdevon.org (accessed 17 August 2019).

References

Blakemore, S J (2018) *Inventing Ourselves: The Secret Life of the Teenage Brain*. London: Doubleday.

Department for Education (DfE) (2018) Keeping Children Safe in Education. [online] Available at: https://assets.publishing.service.gov.uk/government/uploads/system/uploads/attachment_data/file/830121/Keeping_children_safe_in_education_060919.pdf (accessed 19 September 2019).

McCotter, V (2018) Mental Health Green Paper: DfE Update. [online] Available at: www.corc.uk.net/media/1923/vivmccotter-green-paper-presentation-november-2018.pdf (accessed 11 September 2019).

Chapter 6 Proactive prevention models

What? (The big idea)

Jump in! Join in the joy!

The four key barriers to teacher mental well-being and self-care named in *Teacher Recruitment and Retention Strategy* (DfE, 2019) were: workload, support, environment intolerant of change or unable to adapt, and the process of becoming a teacher. It turns out that autonomy and independence of thought are just as critical for teachers as for young people needing to explore their sense of self as they create, break and reform links with a wider and wider community around them. There is something common to pupils and new teachers when faced with the transition from dependence to independence and it is to do with judgement. If our own creation and thought and attempts to try, fail and try again are only judged by others, your own ability to decide for yourself will be compromised.

A profound moment for me was hearing an emotionally challenged trainee teacher tell an incoming cohort that what they need most in order to get through the year is to find their 'inner flexibility'. She said this with such passion and belief – based on first-hand experience – that the whole auditorium took on this mantle as if having been passed a baton. What I really liked about it was that it was richer than the messages about 'resilience', which all too often can be taken destructively to mean 'snap out of it, man up, chin up, button up'. This ties in with Josh Connolly's mantra about children mentioned previously, and it can be applied to teachers too: '[teachers] *are resourceful and whole*' (Murphy, 2019). Sometimes you need to reconnect with your inner strengths and flexibilities.

Dave Roberts talks of the importance of professional supervision for all staff in schools (Roberts, 2017, p 253). This is useful to know where members of staff are expected to demonstrate a level of professionalism which prevents them from swearing when they are angry, from slamming doors when they are upset and from crying when they are exhausted or desperately saddened by a situation at school where a show of human emotion outside the school setting would be expected. It is useful to consider a safe space in school where colleagues can let off steam and offload the emotional baggage they collect around the site each day.

Respecting your physical health needs can support you mentally and vice versa

Visiting our local hospital recently with a lead counsellor from a local school was both enlightening and inspiring. We went along to the hospital's drop-in centre for staff, patients and visitors called 'Here for Health'. It is a relatively new enterprise (just a few years old) and the colleagues there explained to us the range of services they offer – everything from a blood pressure check, to leaflets on well-being, and advice on diet, smoking and exercise. It is proving a resounding success. Figure 6.1 gives a breakdown of the topics discussed by attendees last year.

Oxford University Hospitals NHS

NHS Foundation Trust

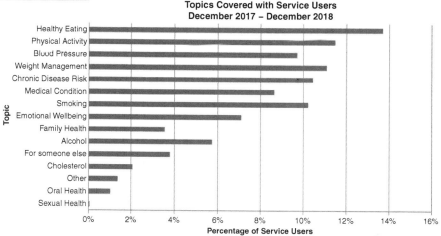

Figure 6.1 Topics covered with service users of Here for Health 2017–18

So what? ◀ ◀ ◀

I have a dream that each secondary school in England will have a 'Here for Health' hub on site. School nurses need to be given the status they deserve and training fit for purpose. This is no longer simply about nits, pregnancy and body odour. The Oxford University Hospital's ground-breaking initiative exemplifies how great institutions can and are responding to societal change in need. Patients, visitors and hospital staff are now at ease with dropping in to Here for Health to gain advice on alcoholism; smoking cessation; blood pressure; sleep hygiene; mental well-being; local exercise or dieting clubs; how to talk with a loved one about dementia, and the list goes on.

Teachers don't have time to go to the doctor. They don't want to leave their classes as they know the importance of routine, especially for the most vulnerable pupils. They feel and are responsible for the learning outcomes of their pupils and so they prioritise their attendance in school above their own health and well-being.

However, instead of role-modelling positive mental and physical self-care, this leads to role-modelling an increasingly stressed and burning-out teacher workforce thinly veiled with a teacher smile so easily seen through by the young sponges in class and in the corridors.

At what point do you deem someone unfit to teach? At what point would you deem a young person too ill to come to school? These questions aren't easy to answer, but I imagine as schools get to grips with the sea change in the benefits of greater mental health awareness and of the links between mental and physical well-being and between these things and behaviour presentations in staffrooms and classrooms, these questions will certainly need to be asked and asked again.

When exploring a societal call for parity between physical and mental health, what can this mean for early career teaching? It could start with the acceptance, de-stigmatisation and normalisation for those entering teaching with pre-existing diagnosed and medicated mental health conditions. The Equal Opportunities Act of 2010, as helpfully elaborated by the Office for Independent Adjudicators, is clear on an employing school's responsibility in providing reasonable adjustment for both mental and physical disabilities. Just *who* is chronically fit to teach, and exactly *when* teachers are justified in calling in sick, is shifting for the better. In the same way that children are finding their place in every classroom to manage their soothe, threat and drive systems (Gilbert, 2005), so too are their teachers.

Table 6.1 A consideration of common physical presentations, effects on the emotional self, preventative measures, curative treatments and possible outcomes

These are taken from live well-being coaching examples from ECT clients with whom I have worked over the last few years.

Physical presentations	Potential effect on emotions within the classroom	Preventative measures	Curative treatments and link to five ways to well-being	Possible outcomes
Headaches/ migraines	Heightened anxiety/ frustration at inability to read/respond normally to light.	Request a room with dimmer lights, a chalkboard instead of projector light, curtains instead of blinds, a fresh current of air moving through it, access to water.	A darkened medical room for school staff as well as for pupils.	Fewer instances of presenteeism or sick leave.
Palpitations	Spiralling anxiety.	Less coffee.	Breathing and walking space during the day.	Reduced heart-rate.
Lethargy/fatigue	Inability to inspire and sustain interest of children with relative hyperactivity.	Engage with self-regulated sleep; have exercise and fresh air during the school day; revisit nutrition and hydration routines.	Journaling a food and drink diary with photos of each meal and snack in order to inform peaks and troughs in energy at home and at school.	Healthier alignment with personal triggers to lethargy and improved self-care and self-respect. Increased engagement with exercise resulting in increased movement in thought and lesson 'spark'.
Sore throat/vocal problems	Lowered mood owing to lowered immunity and increased risk of catching other illnesses as germs move around the school, frustration from lowered connection with pupils.	Hydration; herbal intake; voice-projection coaching; alternative strategies for asking for quiet between tasks (eg a wah-wah tube).	GP visit; increased information about a range of medicines and holistic approaches to curing sore throat and hydration/speech comfort levels owing to occupation.	Increased engagement with colleagues through attendance at free union workshop on voice/ throat management and seasonal/central heating impact on health – role-modelling this information to young people.
Common colds/ fevers/hayfever	Frustration that tasks take longer and marking outside the class is piling up through inability to work in a time-efficient manner.	Note in planner to start each lesson with washing hands ritual and using aromatherapy to soothe nasal passages for self and children in class.	Local honey and non-drowsy hayfever medication to support speedier recovery.	Increased understanding between colleagues and children who also suffer from colds and hayfever – tipsharing on prevention and cure, increasing empathy and respect.

Consider your relationship with medication, alternative solutions, sedation and stimulation to keep you going through the working weeks and terms. Consider the warp and weft of your term and holiday rhythms. Consider how much daylight and fresh air you encounter. How much positive time do you spend with friends and family, really?

Case study ◀◀◀

I know a senior leader who consciously drinks what he describes as too much coffee every day and well after midday. When I asked how on earth he gets to sleep, he replied, 'Oh well that's easy because the wine counteracts the caffeine high and I usually just pass out'.

I know a deputy head in the north of England whose struggle with Sunday evening teacher syndrome (SETS – is this a thing?) is worse than anyone I have heard of to date. She says she knows exactly why she can't sleep on a Sunday night and no matter what she does about it, she knows it won't change. I ask her why. She puts it down to having to deliver the senior leaders' staff briefing every Monday morning. She says it would be fine if it were her briefing notes, but she gets sent them from her leadership colleagues and they aren't her words. A solution seems staring at me in the face – she clearly needs to write her own words in consultation with her leadership colleagues – but this would mean meeting with them prior to 7.00am, which is when she gets into work on Monday to sort through the weekend emails sent by parents and flags which ones need urgent safeguarding attention. Her headteacher sleeps better, she says, because he checks his emails all weekend and responds to them, and gets into work at 6am to pre-empt any knock-on repercussions. She says she refuses to let work eat into her own time. As a result, she cannot sleep on a Sunday night. Ever. Except for holidays – apart from the Sundays before results week, before holiday revision sessions and before Staff INSET returning after holidays. And if there is anything in the press about the school during the holidays. Because children and families don't just have dramas, traumas, accusations and crises in term time.

I know a teacher who has a walking stick. I know a headteacher who failed to shortlist the teacher for a promotion because he felt that the walking stick was a visible sign that the mental health of the teacher was suffering. She talks of propanadol and sertraline and the prescribed medication which pupils are taking to increase focus. Are these sustainable ways of coping? At what point is it useful to consider the reasons behind the need for these crutches and to what extent might this jeopardise current performance? Digging deeper takes time. Some ECTs would rather exist on a level of survival and forfeit the potential to thrive in order to save them the short-term pains this digging deep may take.

How physical symptoms can indicate the need for further mental health supports

NACOA's Josh Connolly is a fan of the body scan and exploring your own internal links between thought, emotion and physical presentations in the wider realm of self-awareness. While Josh is talking about how to support children experiencing anxiety in his six tips YouTube clip (www.youtube.com/watch?=G3OZFDb6TdI), it is clear that for the adults to whom children look for their example, body scanning as part of regular self-awareness checks can bear fruit.

If an ECT suffers from migraines, to what extent do certain classroom situations increase frequency of migraine, or trigger an aura? To what extent can you prevent this by preparative self-care such as sleep regulation, hydration or addressing anxiety around being observed by particular colleagues?

Now what?

Practical task for tomorrow

Ask your class at the start, middle and end of the lesson to put their head in their arms or close their eyes or look somewhere different and think any thoughts they like. Consider your reaction to this experiment, to what extent your mental well-being is affected by it, and whether this type of activity could support your mental well-being within a full teaching day.

Practical task for next week

At the start of the week, make a point of noting your go-to ailments. If you have symptoms linked to chronic mental or physical illness, note when they increase and when they do not. If you have recourse to point-of-need medication, when do you notice yourself taking it more? If you take prescribed medicines regularly, do you ever forget to take them? How does this affect your work, home and social life? How does it affect your relationships with young people, with colleagues, with friends and loved ones?

Practical task for the long term ◀◀◀

Keep a brief note in your planner or school diary of your weekly physical and mental health. List any recurring symptoms: sleeplessness; migraine or headache; lack of appetite or comfort-eating; recourse to alcohol or other relaxants; recourse to caffeine or other stimulants. Reflect regularly on any patterns which emerge. How might you adapt your behaviour to encourage a healthier mind and body?

What next?

Further reading

Gumbrell, D (2019) *Lift! Going Up if Teaching Gets You Down: 39 Reflections to Promote Resilience and Well-Being*. St Albans: Critical Publishing.

Jackson, E (2008) Work Discussion Groups at Work. In Rustin, M and Bradley, J (eds) *Work Discussion: Learning from Reflective Practice in Work with Children and Families* (pp 51–72). London: Karnac.

Lawful, S (2019) Talk presented at NEU Well-being CPD event for Teachers. 24 May 2019. [online] Available at: www.wherethefruitis.co.uk (accessed 11 September 2019).

References

Connolly, J (2019) How to Help a Child with Anxiety. National Association for the Children of Alcoholics. [online] Available at: www.youtube.com/watch?=G30ZFDb6Tdl (accessed 6 August 2019).

Department for Education (DfE) (2019) *Teacher Recruitment and Retention Strategy*. [online] Available at https://assets.publishing.service.gov.uk/government/uploads/system/uploads/attachment_data/file/786856/DFE_Teacher_Retention_Strategy_Report.pdf (accessed 11 September 2019).

Gilbert, P (2005) Compassion and Cruelty: A Biopsychosocial Approach. *Compassion: Conceptualisations, Research and Use in Psychotherapy* (p 26). London: Routledge.

Murphy, H (2019) Take to the Trees. *Omnom*, 3(4): 12–19. [online] Available at www.wherethefruitis.co.uk (accessed 20 August 2019).

Oxford University Hospitals NHS Foundation Trust (nd) Here for Health. [online] Available at: www.ouh.nhs.uk/hereforhealth (accessed 6 August 2019).

Roberts, D (2017) The Importance of Professional Supervision for All Staff in Schools. In Colley, D and Cooper, P (eds) *Attachment and Emotional Development in the Classroom* (pp 233–48). London: Jessica Kingsley.

Chapter 7   When you need more than school colleagues for support

What? (The big idea)

Seek regular advice

Seeking regular advice from a range of trusted sources in support of positive mental health will significantly reduce a teacher's recourse to emergency point-of-need psychiatric intervention.

Actively and overtly engaging with our own mental health needs as an adult is not just important for young people in terms of role-modelling. If the greatest determinant of behavioural choice in young people is the behavioural choice of adults around them, you can usefully role model seeking counsel from a healthy range of people and resources in order to inform your self-care. Giving students live examples of prioritising yourself occasionally will ensure they feel doing the same will be a choice worth making. The role-modelling of self-empowerment is explored fully in the collaborative research between Oxford Brookes University and Family Links (see references).

When learning to become a youth mental health first aid instructor, my mentor Rachel described to us an analogy which has stuck with me and comes out at most training events delivered since! It is widely accepted that, with experience, theory and guidance, it is possible to become a competent and confident driver without needing to be a qualified mechanic. While you might be interested in the workings under the bonnet, to a greater or lesser degree, checking oil, refilling windscreen wash etc, you would usually read or listen to the car's warning signs as a prompt to knowing when to call the mechanic or a specialist. Regular MOT checks are obligatory. In caring for and supporting your own and others' mental health and well-being, you can learn by reading, practice and observation and don't need to be a trained clinician, psychotherapist or counsellor to establish your own competent or confident self-regulation or supportive provision for others. It isn't the number of qualifications in counselling or psychotherapy which matter in preventative engagement with mental well-being and self-care, but the quality of the relationships, either with the self or with the person you are supporting.

This doesn't mean that there are times when medical or specialist support is not needed. None of the above replaces the need for medical assistance; rather, it provides another strand of support as an interim, preventative or parallel measure. Knowing how and when to seek help (Teachers' Standard 8b) can arguably now be seen to extend not only to the remit of challenges an ECT might face with behaviour management, assessment, differentiation, subject knowledge, planning or professional standards, but beyond that to the challenges they might face to do with their own mental well-being and self-care.

An examination of Quadrants 1–4 of MHFA England's Mental Health Continuum leads to greater understanding of the concept that everyone is on the continuum somewhere, whether you are enjoying relative good mental health and well-being and have no diagnosable condition, have poor mental health and no diagnosable condition, have a diagnosis and poor mental health, or you are living with a diagnosed mental health condition yet enjoying good mental health. That your place on the continuum is fluid and that recovery is likely has only relatively recently landed in the understanding of those recruiting and keen to retain ECTs within the teacher workforce. Numerous recent lived experiences from ECTs I work with indicate that there are still ITT providers who will reject or dissuade applicants owing to disclosures of or assumptions around their mental health and preconceptions around how this might affect practice in schools. This not only contravenes the Equal Opportunities Act reforms of 2010, but also signals an affirmation to the applicant that living with a mental health condition bars you from a career in teaching. While the debate surrounding fitness to teach continues, it is arguably advantageous to consider the message that this is sending to young people in schools about diversity and intolerance and about how keeping mental health concerns hidden is role-modelled in front of them on a regular basis.

Indeed, once mental well-being and self-care has improved, it is my experience that the pedagogical challenges faced by ECTs usually seem surmountable too. What mental health first aid is doing as it increasingly pervades school settings is to allow staff the confidence to gauge the level of need (emphatically not to diagnose), offer information, encourage and signpost to professional supports where needed, and encourage other supports.

It is not uncommon that ECTs arrive at their training or employing school with chronic conditions, managed to a greater or lesser extent. Diagnoses can be helpful in supporting ECTs' and their colleagues' knowledge that there are things about them which can't be changed, and therefore blame and fault can be left alone. However, the flipside can be a frustration that these things can't be changed. Flip again, and it could be argued that a disability is part of somebody's persona, and while it doesn't define them, it is part of them.

Imagine how many of your school colleagues are seeking external support in managing their mental health. Double this and add ten. You may be close. The current stigma surrounding mental health is such that school communities can see seeking help as encouraging learned helplessness, as a weakness, as a last-ditch resort accessed by colleagues who aren't suited to teaching, or are at the end of their career. You would hope that all teachers are actively seeking external support but many do not. The more overtly and actively teachers can prioritise their own self-care and well-being, the less likely they will reach a point where they need specialist support. This is separate from those living with chronic and diagnosed conditions for which they are seeking professional help, but reflects a proportion of the wider community who are unwell and, if diagnosed, would be aware of the need for specialist support.

Thankfully, things are changing. Senior leaders in progressive staffrooms are sharing the support they seek. Regular professional supervision for frontline employees working with children (ie the whole-school staff) is currently too expensive to take priority in school budgets. While awaiting the penny-drop moment that regular professional supervision will boost staff morale, increase teacher retention and transform positive mental health promotion for young people within the school community, it can be useful to take time and ask colleagues what they do in order to stay sane; what *their* self-care plan is...

So what? ◀◀◀

What impact can this have on your responses to known triggers?

Schools are right to be prioritising support for ECTs. And the tension comes for where their responsibility begins and yours ends. It is mentally healthy to prioritise your own mental well-being and self-care. If not for yourself, for the young people around you who – whether you like it or not – are looking to you for an alternative role-model. Overtly addressing your own mental health needs; being conscious of when and how to call on others; being conscious of when listening to your own gut is more appropriate – all these things will support young people in building resourcefulness of their own. Being clear that calling on support as one strand of your self-care is a professional strength. This will not only help you, but help others to help you where appropriate and will help young people help themselves.

Spotting the need for support with mental health and what to do about it

Using the five ways to well-being, you can assess your own relative well-being. This set of evidence-based actions recommended by the New Economics Foundation and commissioned by Foresight's Mental Capital and Well-being Project (Aked, 2008) are said to improve personal well-being. This is being taken up by NHS and school organisations to support resourcefulness and positive role-modelling for staff and young people.

Table 7.1 The five ways to well-being for ECTs

Way to well-being	To what extent do you engage with this at school?	To what extent do you engage with this outside school?	To what extent do young people know this about you?	To what extent do you feel this is an area needing more of your attention?
Connect	I take time to chat with colleagues in the staffroom between the end of the school day and starting my marking/planning/parental meetings.	I see elderly relatives every weekend and try to do something fun with friends at least one weeknight and/or one weekend night.	I could chat more with colleagues out in the fresh air – pupils don't often see me not working, or doing something like chatting or laughing with other adults on topics other than work.	I know that I feel quite thinly spread between family and friends and I could do more to encourage non-teaching friends to get why I can't always go out when they do.

Way to well-being	To what extent do you engage with this at school?	To what extent do you engage with this outside school?	To what extent do young people know this about you?	To what extent do you feel this is an area needing more of your attention?
Take notice	Sometimes in the darker months, I literally don't see daylight until the weekend. I know this is bad.	I make a point of getting in the allotment at the weekend.	I could encourage the pupils more to reconnect with nature as they used to at pre-school.	I know that my partner says stuff and I am unable to engage owing to cognitive overload – it's like I need a space between school and home to ditch the school brain.
Keep learning	I always learn from kids in class and colleagues.	When I go to art club it always makes me feel better.	Sometimes I show kids in class what I painted.	This feels pretty healthy.
Be active	I wish we could go outside more to learn.	We try to go swimming or do a long walk as a family each weekend.	The sponsored walk was fun this year – could it be a more frequent school activity?	I'd like to get the motivational warm-up Bollywood guy to come in to school and raise our spirits.

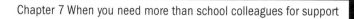

Way to well-being	To what extent do you engage with this at school?	To what extent do you engage with this outside school?	To what extent do young people know this about you?	To what extent do you feel this is an area needing more of your attention?
Give	I feel like I give all the time at school. I could give more smiles maybe and sometimes give myself a break...	We give lots of hugs at home – that's a given!	It's really healthy. I think, to bring in the occasional home-made cake to share.	I think getting the balance right between giving at school and giving in our local community is hard – it feels like you're always being judged, but villagers don't know how much we do at school and vice versa.

Reflective task ◀◀◀

Take a rubber glove and write on each finger and thumb one of the five ways to well-being and an example which you enjoy for each one.

Case study ◀◀◀

Establishing accessible links to professional and other supports

An ECT I worked with had to learn through experience the importance of planning and communication in times of need. She stopped going to school owing to the return of severe depression which had affected her previously. At first, the absence exacerbated her anxiety since the medication she was prescribed was causing her to oversleep and miss the deadline for ringing in sick with colleagues at school.

The anxiety was heightened by the school not getting in touch with her. She felt that they were either justifiably 'sending her to Coventry', or alternatively not caring about her. It turned out that colleagues were simply very busy with the school day and preparing cover for her classes.

When her illness developed to include symptoms of parasuicidal and suicidal behaviour, the school became concerned and visited her home. Paramedics were called and after a spell in A&E, she was given two weeks off work. During this time, her colleagues set up a system by which she could let a named person know if things were deteriorating. In the setting up of these arrangements, she began to realise that the school were definitely supportive, and that only by understanding what she was experiencing could they put in any kind of support plan and access to professional supports which were suited to her needs.

How the choices you make in supporting your role as teacher can affect your performance

If, when trying to address your mental ill-health, you have sought prescriptions for sleeping pills to lower blood pressure, you will have been addressing your mental health needs as a cure. If you have ever laughed at the colleague who goes to their car at lunchtime in order to meditate, or at the teacher who goes swimming at 6am twice a week before school, or at the fellow ECT who never comes to the pub on a Friday after school but chooses to make silver bracelets at jewellery club instead, you may wish to think again.

Now what?

While routines of preventative support to your mental health can make a considerable difference to your job satisfaction and energy levels, there are inevitably times when unexpected challenges meet you head-on. Are you aware of the support out there and how to access it? Having a mental health first aid plan is a good idea as your powers of rational thinking and practical approaches when life serves up its challenges may well be more than compromised.

NACOA worker Josh Connolly provides a convincing argument based on his own lived experience through childhood trauma, addiction and self-managed recovery that everyone is *'naturally resourceful and whole'* and that it is society's responsibility to help the individual find their own resources within.

Practical task for tomorrow ◀◀◀

Take time out for ten minutes and in the left-hand columns, write a list of triggers and symptoms which can affect your mood and ability to function at work. In the right-hand columns, write who you might call on for support and advice and what actions you might take.

Example How seeking support can be professional and solution-focused

Trigger	Symptom	Advice from...	Action	Outcome
Colleague absence	Feel quality of learning in own class is compromised owing to having to set cover for other classes.	Line manager	Have stock of self-marking, discrete cover packs ready if needed.	Less resentful of colleague's need for self-care and feel better about asking for own time off when needed.
Sleepless night	Cognitive skills slowing down.	Staffroom colleagues	Try sleeping tips: no gadgets one hour before bed; cup of tea; 4-7-8 breathing (Fletcher, 2019).	Sleep improves; brain works more efficiently at work.
TA seems snappy	Need to take on more tasks you'd normally ask TA to do – to save time.	Pupils	Thank TA for all he does and give him a break for start of Tues morning class as he comes straight from breakfast club to lesson on that day.	Pupils' opinion valued; TA less snappy; more positive atmosphere in class.
Traffic made me late again	Started off day in bad mood.	Headteacher	Apply for staff cycle scheme and try this on heavily congested days.	Fitter routine; headteacher feels useful; easier emotional regulation to start the day.

Practical task for next week ◀◀◀

Reflect over the next week about who the four most trusted and useful people you have around you who you call on in times of need (Jung, 2003). Consider which of them represents the *lover* archetype: someone with whom you share reciprocal love and understanding and complete trust (it can be a partner, relative or close friend); consider which represents the *elder* archetype: someone with considerably more life experience than yourself who will offer wisdom; consider who represents the *wizard* archetype for you – someone who will offer an unexpected perspective, challenge you in a novel or refreshing way or approach your challenge from a new and eye-opening viewpoint; consider who represents the *warrior* archetype for you: someone who knows you well enough not to collude with your woes, but who will hold you to account and challenge you to fight and stretch yourself.

- Take another rubber glove or draw around your hand on card. Consider who your four go-to people are and what types of challenge would be good for them to hear about and advise on. Remember, try to choose people who can offer you a unique perspective: are they one of the Jungian archetypal figure type (Jung, 2003)?

>> elder – thinking;

>> lover – feeling;

>> wizard – sensation;

>> warrior – intuition.

- Write one name on each finger. The thumb of the glove is reserved for the person who knows you best of all. Remember that you are naturally resourceful and whole. On the thumb, write 'me'.

Practical tasks for the long term ◀◀◀

Youth and Adult Mental Health First Aid teaches us the ALGEE action plan and this has been adopted and re-worded by Young Minds Advocacy. (I recommend you consider asking your school setting to invest in Youth MHFA training for you.) It could usefully also be applied as ECT advocacy: assess for risk of suicide or harm; listen non-judgementally; give information, comfort and reassurance; encourage appropriate professional help; encourage self-help and other supports for the individual and for friends and family around them.

- Take ten minutes with your line manager to share signposting tips. Ask your well-being officer or HR manager what local and recommended support there is for teachers in times of need. Ask your union rep too.

- Taking an hour a month to reflect on the highs and lows and the circumstances in which they arose can help you plan effectively for the month ahead. Keep refreshing, updating and adding to your signposting list.

What next? ◀ ◀ ◀

Further reading

Davis, S et al (2019) *Mental Health First Aid (MHFA) England Impact Report 2018–19.* [online] Available at: www.mhfaengland.org (accessed 17 August 2019).

Hub of Hope (nd) [online] Available at: www.hubofhope.co.uk (accessed 17 August 2019).

Hussain, M (2019) A Muslim Perspective on Living Well with Good Mental Health. In Fletcher, J (ed) *Chaplaincy and Spiritual Care in Mental Health Settings.* London: Jessica Kingsley.

Morgan, A J, Ross, A and Reavley, N J (2018) Systematic Review and Meta-Analysis of MHFA Training: Effects on Knowledge, Stigma, and Helping Behaviour. *PLOS ONE,* 13(5): e0197102. https://doi.org/10.1371/journal.pone.0197102

Narayanasamy, M, Geraghty, J, Coole, C, Nouri, F, Thomson, L, Callaghan P and Drummond, A (2018) *MENTal Health First Aid in The WORkplace (MENTOR): A Feasibility Study.* Nottingham: IOSH, University of Nottingham.

Oxford University Hospitals NHS Foundation Trust (nd) Here for Health. [online] Available at: www.ouh.nhs.uk/patient-guide/here-for-health/default.aspx (accessed 17 August 2019).

Reavley, N J, Morgan, A, Fischer, J, Kitchener, B, Bovopoulos, N and Jorm A (2018) *Effectiveness of eLearning and Blended Modes of Delivery of Mental Health First Aid Training in the Workplace: Randomised Controlled Trial.* Melbourne: Centre for Mental Health, Melbourne School of Population and Global Health.

River Leadership (nd) [online] Available at: www.riverleadership.org (accessed 17 August 2019).

Rock, C (2017) A Flexible Approach for Improving Mental Health Care in Schools. [online] Available at: www.youngmindsadvocacy.org (accessed 6 August 2019).

References

Aked, J (2008) *Five Ways to Well-being: The Evidence*. [online] Available at: https://neweconomics.org/2008/10/five-ways-to-wellbeing-the-evidence (accessed 11 September 2019).

Family Links (nd) *Evaluation of Family Links Transforming Learning Workshops*. Research report delivered as part of Initial Teacher Education at Oxford Brookes University. [online] Available at: www.familylinks.org.uk (accessed 6 August 2019).

Fletcher, J (2019) How to Use 4-7-8 Breathing for Anxiety. *Medical News Today*, 11 February. [online] Available at: www.medicalnewstoday.com (accessed 6 August 2019).

Jung, C (2003) *Four Archetypes: Psychological Types*. 3rd edn. London: Routledge.

Sources of support

www.hubofhope.co.uk	An updated online directory of local mental health supports by postcode.
www.talkingspaceplus.org.uk	Free NHS service for online mental health support.
www.educationsupportpartnership.org.uk	UK charity dedicated to improving the health and well-being of teachers, teaching assistants, head teachers, lecturers and support staff in schools.
www.mentalhealth.org.uk	Research-based support for mental health online including resources for teachers, parents and young people.
www.annafreud.org	Anna Freud National Centre for Children and Families is a children's charity dedicated to providing training and support for child mental health services.
www.silvercloudhealth.com	Mental health solutions developed with over 15 years of research to empower patients to receive effective iCBT in the comfort and privacy of their own homes.
www.getconnected.org.uk	A free online support source for under 25 year-olds.
www.sane.org.uk	SANE is a leading UK mental health charity improving quality of life for anyone affected by mental illness – including family friends and carers.

www.thecalmzone.net	The Campaign Against Living Miserably (CALM) is leading a movement against suicide, the single biggest killer of men under 45 in the UK.
www.mind.org.uk	An online support for mental health focussed on support and respect for those in need and critical need.
www.youngminds.org.uk	A website devoted to supporting young people living with mental health distress, and to supporting those around them.
www.samaritans.org	A free 24 hour service for support with challenges which can be faced by anyone at any time.

Chapter 8   Prioritising gratitude

What? (The big idea)

Think of thanks!

A well-respected and highly driven senior leader with whom I started teaching as an NQT has a self-care routine which is highly polished – he coaches rugby at the weekends, makes the most of every school holiday, is highly boundaried, loyal to friends and family and direct about his needs and intentions to colleagues at every turn. In his first few years, he would give assemblies on positivity and making the most of life, appreciating and grasping opportunity at every turn. At university, he was having a 'shocker' of a time and could have entered the path of self-pity, idleness and coasting. His good friend discovered that he was facing terminal illness and yet still managed to see the positive in everything, up to the end. So, even now, probably subconsciously, this senior leader takes time to be thankful for what he has, faces challenges as opportunities and procrastinates very little.

Through Imam Monawar Hussain's writing on a Muslim perspective on living well with good mental health it is easy to understand the benefits of an open mind when contemplating the virtues of tolerance within school communities. Because the ECT workforce is made up of an increasingly healthy range of physically, ethnically, generationally and neurologically diverse individuals, it is worth exploring the benefits of appreciation through the heart, the spoken word and in deed. I have worked in schools where mentors, senior staff, ECTs, parents, school staff and young learners have designated time to the overt and regular practice of gratitude, celebrating the successes of individuals for who they are and for what they bring to the community. Those schools are paving the way for an increased sense of belonging and are encouraging retention and dedication.

When starting out in a new school setting, there are silent laws for an ECT to absorb, just as for schoolchildren (Bourdieu, 1992, p 199). Bourdieu's 'doxa' theory, of that which is unspoken and accepted – the unwritten expectations of colleagues – about the environment in which you live, is something of a tricky initiation and a rite of passage which traditionally can leave new teachers scathed (they sit in the wrong chair in the staffroom, for example). This is one reason why engaging with an appropriate body and teaching union for support and advice, establishing a channel of communication prior to any potential challenges, is healthy. Constructing daily periods of conscious gratitude can support recovery from embarrassing faux-pas and reduce relapses of periods of mental ill health.

Societal acceptance of cognitive behavioural therapy and positive self-talk both inwardly and to others sits awkwardly with a traditional English mindset of self-deprecation. However, the benefits of acknowledging success and taking notice of achievements, balancing judgement with recognition, are accepted within emotionally intelligent school staffrooms.

This chapter explores Mike Culley's research. Mike is an occupational psychologist in education who spoke at the NEU's Promoting Teachers' Mental Health and Well-being conference in March 2018 on the importance of taking regular time to be grateful for the positives within our working and home lives. This, in turn, can re-train a disillusioned new teacher's mindset to approach challenges with a positive rather than defeatist attitude to their practice. This can transform the inability to accept a negative comment from lesson feedback or parental consultation into a solution-focused mindset which embraces this same feedback constructively.

So what? ◀ ◀ ◀

This means that taking care over your perspective before looking to judge failures in teaching and planning can reduce workload and improve working relationships.

Table 8.1 How approaches to practice can impact positively

	Consider	Communicate
Consult www.atmybest. com and complete the free online task to consider your strengths at school and during free time.	One of your colleagues who you can struggle to relate to. What strengths do they demonstrate at school and what do you believe to be true for them during their free time?	Take some time to be grateful for the qualities your colleague brings to the organisation. Monitor how your perception of them and your relationship with them changes.
Consider which strengths you would have chosen as a pupil when you were at school.	One of your pupils who you can struggle to relate to. What strengths do they demonstrate in the wider school and what do you believe to be true for them during their free time?	Take some time to acknowledge the contribution they make to the wider school community. Monitor how your perception of them and your relationship with them changes.
Consider what you perceive your parenting strengths to be (if not a parent, imagine you are).	One parent or carer who you can struggle to relate to. What strengths do you believe them to demonstrate within their community?	Take some time to acknowledge the contribution they make within their community. Monitor how your perception of them and your relationship with them changes.

Reflective task ◀◀◀

- Consider a lesson which didn't go well and/or a colleague with whom you struggle to see eye-to-eye.

- Note down some facts which indicate the negative thoughts you have about the lesson or colleague.

- Reflect on how things could have gone better.

- What would have had to happen for you to have positive thoughts about that lesson or colleague?

Case study ◀◀◀

Applying your gratitude skills to help focus on solutions

In Chapter 2, Sami's development to becoming a positive and respected practitioner was explored. He endured many trials which almost got the better of his confidence in continuing his teacher training and completing QTS. In the darkest times, Sami experienced frequent mornings of extreme anxiety in which he struggled and often failed to get out of bed and go to school. He read a great deal during his break from teaching practice and taught himself to reconfigure his inner self-talk. Anxiety over the pending school day became excitement; challenge became opportunity. He practised a daily gratitude ritual to enable him to convert his reluctance to go to school into eager anticipation of the school day ahead.

Now what? ◀ ◀ ◀

From challenge to opportunity

Practical task for tomorrow ◀◀◀

Think of one child or colleague who has a habit of frustrating you. Engineer an interaction with them which starts by you thanking them. Don't prolong the interaction too long. Consider their response and then reflect on how this makes you feel.

Practical task for next week ◀◀◀

As you wake up on Monday morning, consider how you are feeling. If the sinking feeling of it being Monday and no longer the weekend comes, try to replace the anxiety and dread by telling yourself: 'I'm so grateful for the opportunity to try today. And if it doesn't go so well, I'm grateful that I can try again, having learned from the mistakes I might make today. Not only will I learn from those mistakes, but the pupils in class today will see that nobody's perfect and that is a great lesson to learn.'

Practical task for the long term ◀ ◀ ◀

Assign your own mental well-being and self-care principles and remind yourself and those closest around you on a regular basis what those principles are. Here are some examples.

1. Respect the context of your early career.

2. Encourage collaboration over isolation.

3. Balance judgement with recognition of achievement.

4. Expect an individual plan of self-care, role-modelling where necessary.

5. Expect continuing professional development to require support, mentoring or coaching.

6. Ask yourself the following simple questions (as advocated by Youth Mental Health First Aid) as part of a regular self-care routine to support self-assessment of level of need:

   a) Do you have evidence to support your feelings?

   b) What can you change?

   c) What can't you change and need to accept?

   d) What needs your urgent attention?

   e) Can anyone help you?

I am increasingly seeing best practice where whole-school well-being policies are taking into account the needs of all areas of staff – from those nearing retirement to those recently appointed. The policy is visible in all areas of the school, and where challenges arise between colleagues reference is made back to these principles as a matter of course when looking for solutions. Here are some examples.

1. ECT receives parental complaint – line manager supports response, respecting the context of the early career and reassures the ECT that mistakes are part of the job. They draft a response with the ECT, given their extensive knowledge of the parental situation and window on the world.

2. Peer review feedback identifies planning as an area for development in the

ECT's non-specialist classes (ECT teaches across three subjects within one faculty). Action plan includes co-planning time with experienced subject lead to support and develop planning.

3. Work scrutiny singles out ECT marking not yet reflecting school marking policy – head of key stage reminds senior leadership team of ECT contribution to new phonics assessment procedures and time-saving EHCP review system and sets up senior leader and ECT co-marking PPA in order to model smart-marking strategies.

4. ECT is working from 7am until 7pm every day at school, except Friday, when they run an after-school club. Headteacher checks in with the ECT at lunchtime when not on duty and suggests a walk off-site to compare well-being strategies and encourage strategic disengagement during non-directed time.

5. Induction mentor has listed ECT as at risk of failing induction owing to shortcomings in behaviour management. Appropriate body visits school and reminds the ECT and employing school that targeted coaching in areas for development are expectations of the induction period and negotiates a combination of observation, support and further developmental coaching. The ECT observes experienced colleagues with specific focus relating to maintaining focus in plenary phase of learning segment.

Well-being and self-care benefits of reading

It is refreshing to know that taking time to read a little can support some challenging times and help you see the funny side. Above all, I am grateful for friends and colleagues such as the author of a recent TES article who give us respite from a sometimes harrowing job with a little humour and hope. Speaking on the benefits of ignoring older teachers a little more, he says:

> *Being aged does not, in itself, confer on us the wisdom of Solomon, and yet too many younger colleagues listen to us for way too long. We are just as likely to be wrong and misguided as they are. I still make the same mistakes in my work as I did at 25 – I just make them more slowly.*
>
> (Petty, 2019)

It is reading such things from such people that give hope that, despite the challenges and infuriations of this extraordinary profession, it is possible, still, to have a long and happy teaching career. In conclusion, I would like to prioritise gratitude in thanking you for choosing to read part or all of this guide and thank you for the contribution you make to children's lives. You are worth it. Believe in yourself!

What next?

Further reading

Culley, M (2018) Paper presented at the NEU Promoting Teacher Wellbeing regional conference, March 2018. [online] Available at: www.mikeculley.uk (accessed 20 August 19).

Hussain, M (2019) A Muslim Perspective on Living Well with Good Mental Health. In Fletcher, J (ed) *Chaplaincy and Spiritual Care in Mental Health Settings*. London: Jessica Kingsley.

Palacio, J (nd) Digital Therapuetics for Mental Health Shown as Effective Intervention for Severe Presentations of Depression and Anxiety. [online] Available at: www.silvercloudhealth.com (accessed 11 September 2019).

Pervez, A (2014) The Concept of Thankfulness in Islam. [online] Available at: www.whyislam.org/on-faith/the-concept-of-gratitude-in-islam (accessed 20 August 19).

Reklau, M (2018) *The Life-changing Power of Gratitude: 7 Simple Exercises That Will Change Your Life for the Better*. USA: Author.

References

Bourdieu, P (1992) Doxa and Common Life. *New Left Review*, 191: 111–21.

Petty, S (2019) Older Teachers Need to be Ignored a Bit More. *TES*, 28 June. [online] Available at: www.tes.com/news/older-teachers-need-be-ignored-bit-more (accessed 17 August 2019).

Acronym buster

Acronym	What does it stand for?	Notes/links
A&E	Accident and Emergency	Department of hospital
AB	Appropriate body	Organisation responsible for quality assurance in Newly Qualified Teacher induction at their employing school
ALGEE	Approach; Listen; Give support and information; Encourage professional support; Encourage other support for the person, for their friends and family	Mental Health First Aid England guidelines for supporting someone in a mental health first aid situation www.mhfaengland.org
AOB	Any other business	For example, on a meeting agenda
BACP	British Association for Counselling and Psychotherapy	www.bacp.co.uk/
CBT	Cognitive behavioural therapy	
CCG	Clinical Commissioning Groups	
CPD	Continuing professional development	
CPSQ	Cambridge Personal Style Questionnaire	
DBT	Dialectical behaviour therapy	
DfE	Department for Education	www.gov.uk/government/ organisations/ department-for-education
DSA	Disabled Students' Allowance	
DSL	Designated safeguarding lead	
DT	Design and technology	
ECF	Early Career Framework	
ECT	Early career teacher	
EHCP	Education and Health Care Plan	
GDPR	General Data Protection Regulation	

Acronym	What does it stand for?	Notes/links
GP	General practitioner (doctor)	
HR	Human resources	
INSET	In-service training	
ITT	Initial Teacher Training	
LAC	Looked after child	
MAT	Multi-academy trust	
MBTI	Myers–Briggs Type Indicator	
MHFA	Mental Health First Aid	www.mhfaengland.org
MOT	Ministry of Transport	
NACOA	National Association for Children of Alcoholics	www.nacoa.org.uk
NASBTT	National Association of School-Based Teacher Trainers	www.nasbtt.org.uk
NEF	New Economics Foundation	https://neweconomics.org
NEU	National Education Union	https://neu.org.uk
NHS	National Health Service	
NQT	Newly Qualified Teacher	
OIA	Office for Independent Adjudicators	
ONS	Office for National Statistics	
OUH	Oxford University Hospitals	
16PF	16 personality factor tool	
PPA	Planning, preparation and assessment time	
PRU	Pupil Referral Unit	
PTA	Parent Teacher Association	
QTS	Qualified Teacher Status	
RSE	Relationships and sex education	
SCITT	School-centred Initial Teacher Training	

Acronym	What does it stand for?	Notes/links
SDIP	School Development and Improvement Plan	
SDQ	Strengths and Difficulties Questionnaire	
SEND	Special Educational Needs and Disability	
SLT	Senior leadership team	
SMART	Specific, measurable, agreed upon, realistic, time-based	Usually referring to objectives/ goals
TA	Teaching assistant	
TES	*Times Educational Supplement*	
TS	Teachers' Standards	www.gov.uk/government/ publications/teachers-standards
UCET	Universities Council for the Education of Teachers	www.ucet.ac.uk
WISE	Well-being in Secondary Education (University of Bristol ongoing project)	www.bristol.ac.uk/population-health-sciences/projects/wise/background.html
WRAP	Wellness Recovery Action Plan (Mental Health First Aid, England)	https://mhfaengland.org

Index